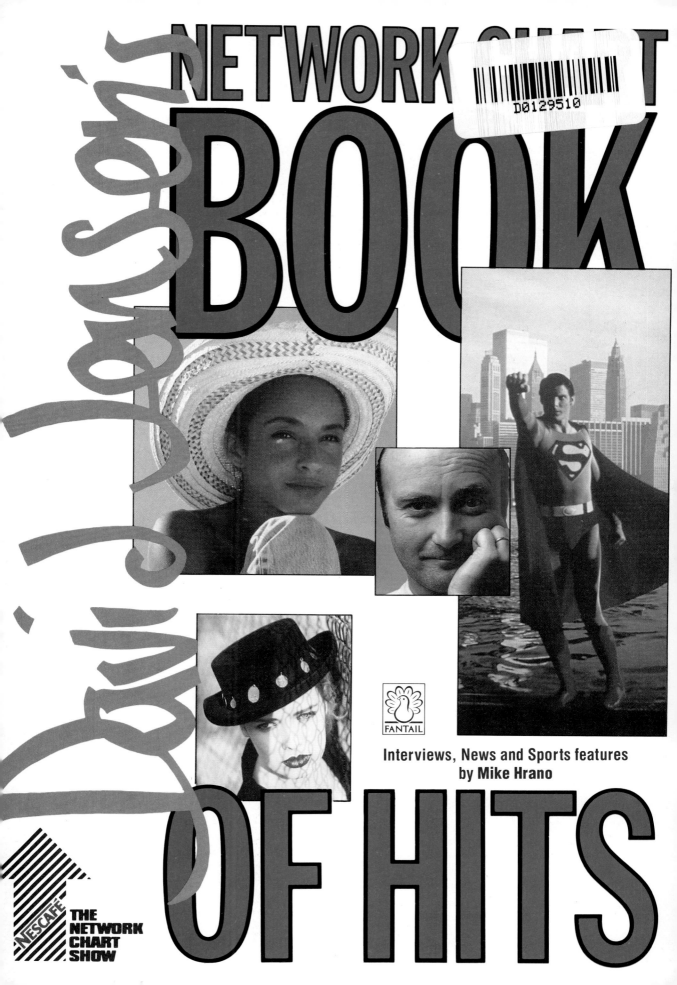

NETWORK CHART
BOOK
OF HITS

David Jensen

D0129510

FANTAIL

Interviews, News and Sports features
by **Mike Hrano**

NESCAFÉ
THE NETWORK CHART SHOW

Title Page photo credits:
Superman – Rex Features
Sade – Chris Roberts
Phil Collins – Retna
Kim Wilde – Retna

FANTAIL PUBLISHING
an imprint of Puffin Enterprises.

Art Directed by Dave Crook

Designed and Typeset by Decode Design

Published by the Penguin Group,
27 Wrights Lane,
London W8 5TZ,
England.

First published 1989.

13579108642

0140900241

Note: Since the album and video charts do not generally change as
       frequently or as drastically as the singles charts, only the
       album and video charts from the first week of each month have
       been printed.

Printed and bound in Great Britain by
William Clowes Limited, Beccles and London

THE NETWORK CHART SHOW

The Network Chart is Britain's fastest and most accurate music survey brought to you live every week on the Independent Radio network.

Every Sunday between 5pm and 7pm, 43 Independent Radio Stations are linked up from Southampton to Scotland, from Cardiff to Belfast, so no matter where you live in Britain it is almost certain that you can receive the show.

The Network Chart is now in its fifth year of compilation and broadcast. Instigated by Independent Radio and MRIB in September 1984, the chart is unique in the UK in combining singles sales – records that are bought by you in your local record store, together with singles airplay – those records you hear on your local Independent Radio station. Each week MRIB collects sales figures from the reports from record retailers throughout the United Kingdom including returns from major chains and specialist independent radio outlets. New playlist information from participating Independent Radio Stations is also gathered on a weekly basis. These two sets of figures are then integrated within the MRIB computer system, matching sales to airplay for each title resulting in a totally up-to-date pop hit list. The result is the chart you hear every Sunday presented by one of Britain's most experienced broadcasters, David Jensen.

Canadian-born David has been broadcasting since he was at school in Vancouver, and moved to Radio Luxembourg when he was only 16. Because of his extreme youth, David became known as "The Kid". From Luxembourg he moved to Radio One and then on to Capital Radio where he now hosts his own daily programme and the Network Chart Show.

Timing is absolutely crucial in broadcasting the chart to the network which means David, his producer and team are preparing the records for the week's run-down well before the start at 5pm. Lists are checked and double-checked, the commercials are lined up and it's all systems go on the dot of five o'clock.

The Network Chart is sponsored by Nescafé, an agreement which made history in 1986 when it started as the first directly sponsored item in a commercial radio programme. As a result of the success of the chart show the Network Chart Show has toured the country and spin-offs such as sweatshirts and T-shirts have become very popular.

Finally, it isn't just Britain that considers the Network Chart as the fastest and most accurate music survey. The show is also carried by over a score of radio stations around the world including Denmark, Japan, New Zealand, Monaco, Columbia and Dubai, adding many millions of listeners to those already hearing the show in the UK.

JANUARY

NETWORK CHART TOP 40

1	ALWAYS ON MY MIND	Pet Shop Boys	(Parlophone)
2	FAIRYTALE OF NEW YORK	Pogues & Kirsty MacColl	(Pogue Mahone)
3	WHEN I FALL IN LOVE	Nat King Cole	(Capitol)
4	HEAVEN IS A PLACE ON EARTH	Belinda Carlisle	(Virgin)
5	LOVE LETTERS	Alison Moyet	(CBS)
6	MY ARMS KEEP MISSING YOU	Rick Astley	(RCA)
7	ANGEL EYES	Wet Wet Wet	(Precious Organisation)
8	HOUSE ARREST	Krush	(Club)
9	ROCKIN' AROUND THE CHRISTMAS TREE	Mel Smith & Kim Wilde	(10)
10	EVERY TIME WE SAY GOODBYE	Simply Red	(Elektra)
11	CHINA IN YOUR HAND	T'Pau	(Siren)
12	THE WAY YOU MAKE ME FEEL	Michael Jackson	(Epic)
13	JINGO	Jellybean	(Chrysalis)
14	TURN BACK THE CLOCK	Johnny Hates Jazz	(Virgin)
15	I FOUND SOMEONE	Cher	(Geffen)
16	STUTTER RAP	Morris Minor & The Majors	(10)
17	WHO FOUND WHO	Jellybean & Elisa Fiorillo	(Chrysalis)
18	WHAT DO YOU WANT TO MAKE...	Shakin' Stevens	(Epic)
19	TOUCHED BY THE HAND OF GOD	New Order	(Factory)
20	THE LOOK OF LOVE	Madonna	(Sire)
21	COME INTO MY LIFE	Joyce Sims	(London)
22	CRITICISE	Alexander O'Neal	(Tabu)
23	LETTER FROM AMERICA	Proclaimers	(Chrysalis)
24	CHILDREN SAY	Level 42	(Polydor)
25	IDEAL WORLD	The Christians	(Island)
26	GTO	Sinitta	(Fanfare)
27	GOT MY MIND SET ON YOU	George Harrison	(Dark Horse)
28	TIGHTEN UP	Wally Jump Junior & Criminal Element	(Breakout)
29	FATHER FIGURE	George Michael	(Epic)
30	RISE TO THE OCCASION	Climie Fisher	(EMI)
31	THERE'S THE GIRL	Heart	(Capitol)
32	MY BABY JUST CARES FOR ME	Nina Simone	(Charly)
33	ONCE UPON A LONG AGO	Paul McCartney	(Parlophone)
34	IN GOD'S COUNTRY	U2	(Island)
35	SO EMOTIONAL	Whitney Houston	(Arista)
36	NEVER CAN SAY GOODBYE	Communards	(London)
37	PACK JAMMED	Stock Aitken Waterman	(Breakout)
38	SATELLITE	Hooters	(CBS)
39	SOMEBODY LOVED ME	Smiths	(Rough Trade)
40	THE WISHING WELL	Gosh!	(MBS)

Sinitta

George Michael

(EPIC)

JANUARY

NUMBER 1 ONE ACT

THE PET SHOP BOYS

(RETNA)

Chris Lowe and Neil Tennant have made being boring interesting, and deadpanned their way to an uninterrupted flow of top ten hits in the process.

The Pet Shop Boys have been called the most miserable men in pop, but it was their cheery privilege to enjoy the first number one single of 1988. "Always On My Mind", an Eighties update of the Seventies hit for Elvis Presley, held the pole position in the Network Chart over the New Year break - and gave the downcast duo a third British chart-topper.

The first had come just two years earlier, when "West End Girls" announced the arrival of a new pop group decidely different from so many of the grinning, bouncing bands which had gone before. The feat was repeated with "It's A Sin", then again following "Always On My Mind", with "Heart". But not for Chris and Neil the contented, ear to ear grins of success, and it has always been that way - ever since Neil first advised his partner not to look "too triumphant" on the occasion of their first appearance on TV.

"When we first started making records, we didn't want to be like other pop groups," Neil explains. "We always tried to have an image that was unpopstar-ish and quite stern. We also presented ourselves in a detached way, so that we are not quite real in what we do. We didn't want to be smiling, goodtime party people - because we weren't interested in that kind of thing. Besides, I'm getting old. I'm 34 - I can't leap around like George Michael and smile all the time!"

Instead, the Pet Shop Boys have simply stood there, expressionless, as the hits keep coming. The very epitome of two men brilliantly unimpressed by the claiming of fame.

Neil and Chris – cheery chappies!

(RETNA)

Neil and Chris – full of fun!

Indeed, that dismissive stance has succeeded in causing offence to many dedicated followers of the pop scene. So when Neil appeared yawning on the cover of "Actually", the third Pet Shop Boys' album, it was widely held that he had taken the joke a little too far. "I thought the cover was very funny," he shrugs, "but some people took it really personally. It wasn't meant to be blase..."

Much of what the Pet Shop Boys do often seems that way but, from the very beginning, Chris and Neil have carefully structured their career and seized the right opportunities to advance themselves artistically and with integrity.

They first met when Chris, who was busy doing a degree in architecture at Liverpool University, was trying to get his guitar mended at an electronics shop in the Kings Road, London. Neil walked in, they began chatting, and found they had a lot in common - chiefly the fact that they both wanted to become pop stars.

As a music journalist, Neil had certainly come into contact with enough of them, and felt he could do better than most. It was in 1983, during an assigment to interview Sting from The Police in New York, that he decided to do something drastic about it. He rang up Bobby 'O' Orlando, an American disco producer whom he had long admired, invited him out to lunch - and handed him a demo tape of some songs. Bobby liked what he heard, Chris and Neil signed to his production company and the Pet Shop Boys were on their way.

Except that, after he had given up the security of his job as Assistant Editor of Smash Hits, Neil found that their first single had been a spectacular flop. Of course, the re-release of "West End Girls" fared rather better, and since then the group has gone on to pick up awards and score hits all over the world with apparent ease - leaving them both as bemused as ever.

"Even if we wanted to, we'd never be big stars," says Chris. "We have no star quality. We're the kind of people nobody remembers. At school, not a single teacher managed to remember my name."

These days, millions of people do know who Chris Lowe is, but some things never change, says Neil. Like state of mind. "Just because you're at number one, it doesn't mean you have to be in a good mood...

OUT OF THIS WORLD

For the best part of a year, Yuri Romanenko literally disappeared off the face of the planet - and came home a record-breaker.

The Russian cosmonaut spent a world-beating 326 days in space, and when he made his first public appearance in January following the spectacular voyage, nobody would have blinked an eyelid had his first words to the assembled media been "Hello, earthlings." Instead, the lonesome traveller uttered something even more remarkable: "I feel fine."

Three small words, perhaps, but potentially one giant sentence for mankind. For the significance of Romanenko's physical and mental condition on returning home has far-reaching implications in the field of space travel. It brings the possibility of manned misisons to Mars considerably nearer to reality.

Until Romanenko's marathon jaunt, it had been widely held that the health of cosmonauts would seriously deteriorate in the extended weightlessness of the 30-month, round trip voyage. But his comments have - in the minds of many, if not all - altered that line of thinking. Romanenko reported that he suffered virtually no ill effects from his long flight. In the past, Soviet cosmonauts have returned from long missions with bones, muscles and cardio-vascular systems weakened by extended periods in zero gravity.

Romanenko claimed he could stand up, albeit shakily, shortly after his Soyuz capsule touched down in Soviet Kazakhstan. "My muscles were strong enough to support me," he said. "As far as palpitations, sweating and that sort of thing were concerned - I didn't feel anything of the sort. In fact, one day after returning to earth, I went for my first jog - for about 100 metres."

The race is now on between the Russians and the Americans to take man a rather more considerable distance...

Yuri Romanenko – boldly going where no man had stayed so long before.

(ASSOCIATED PRESS)

SUPERBOWL

It was to be a clash of the Titans; two mountains of men coming face to face in the annual sporting spectacle of the "American Way".

As the final countdown to Superbowl XXII got underway, all attention was focused on two of American football's superstars of the moment. One was John Elway of the Denver Broncos, 6ft 3in, fair-haired - and considered by many to be the best quarterback of this century. The other was Dexter Manley of the Washington Redskins, 6ft 5ins, 18 stone - whose unenviable task it was to stop Elway making an even bigger name for himself.

And the pre-match build-up to the big day on January 31 was equally impressive. "We both have nice smiles," explained the Redskins number 72 , "but only one of us will be flashing white teeth - and that's going to be Dexter Manley. I rate Elway as one of the best players around, but I'm pretty good too, and if I don't get to him, we lose."

Having been on the losing side himself in the previous year's Superbowl - when the Broncos were hammered 39-20 by the New York Giants - Elway was not about to be got at. He remained sensibly silent at the time, preferring to save his energy for out there on the grid, but his team mate - wide-receiver Ricky Nattiel - made sure the Redskins camp knew what they would be up against.

"To be honest, the strength of John's arm is scary," he warned. "The first time I ran for him and caught the ball, he almost broke my finger. I had to have a splint on it for about a week."

So the scene was set for a major battle at the Jack Murphy Stadium in San Diego to be fought out before 74,000 cheering spectators, 130 million Americans watching it on TV - and millions more glued to their TV and radio sets back in Britain.

And the result? Against the odds, Elway - the game's highest-paid player - failed to win the day, and the Redskins scored a convincing 42-10 victory. Dexter Manley's smile had never been so bright.

(ALLSPORT)

The Redskins take a few more scalps.

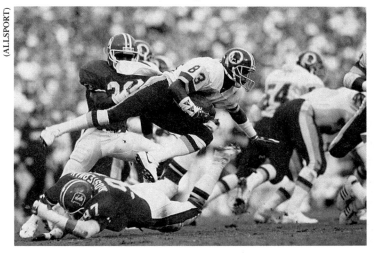

TOP 10 MUSIC VIDEOS

This Week	Last Week	Title	Artist	Label
1	1	CV	Peter Gabriel	(Virgin)
2	5	THE SINGLES	The Pretenders	(WEA)
3	7	NOW THAT'S WHAT I CALL MUSIC 10	Various	(PMI/Virgin)
4	3	MAGIC YEARS - THE COMPLETE SET	Queen	(PMI)
5	9	LIVE	Eurythmics	(Polygram)
6	2	HITS 7	Various	(CBS/Fox)
7	4	BETWEEN THE LINES	Five Star	(PMI)
8	12	THE BEST OF UB40	UB40	(Virgin)
9	6	ONCE UPON A VIDEO	Paul McCartney	(PMI)
10	15	LIVE UNDER A BLOOD RED SKY	U2	(Virgin)

TOP 20 ALBUMS

This Week	Last Week	Title	Artist	Label
1	1	NOW THAT'S MUSIC	Various	(EMI/Virgin/Polygram)
2	5	WHENEVER YOU NEED SOMEBODY	Rick Astley	(RCA)
3	3	BAD	Michael Jackson	(Epic)
4	2	HITS 7	Various	(CBS/WEA/RCA/Arista)
5	9	ACTUALLY	Pet Shop Boys	(Parlophone)
6	7	TANGO IN THE NIGHT	Fleetwood Mac	(Warner Brothers)
7	20	POPPED IN SOULED OUT	Wet Wet Wet	(Precious Organisation)
8	4	BRIDGE OF SPIES	T'Pau	(Siren)
9	24	THE CHRISTIANS	The Christians	(Chrysalis)
10	6	ALL THE BEST	Paul McCartney	(Parlophone)
11	10	THE SINGLES	The Pretenders	(Sire)
12	23	YOU CAN DANCE	Madonna	(Sire)
13	25	LIFE IN THE FAST LANE	Various	(Telstar)
14	56	JACK MIX '86-'88	Mirage	(Stylus)
15	14	FAITH	George Michael	(Epic)
16	26	THE HARDLINE ACCORDING TO...	Terence Trent D'Arby	(CBS)
17	22	WHITNEY	Whitney Houston	(Arista)
18	19	WHITESNAKE 1987	Whitesnake	(EMI)
19	8	RAINDANCING	Alison Moyet	(CBS)
20	18	THE BEST OF UB40	UB40	(DEP International)

TOP 10 SINGLES

WEEK 2

This Week	Last Week	Title	Artist	Label
1	4	HEAVEN IS A PLACE ON EARTH	Belinda Carlisle	(Virgin)
2	1	ALWAYS ON MY MIND	Pet Shop Boys	(Parlophone)
3	8	HOUSE ARREST	Krush	(Club)
4	16	STUTTER RAP	Morris Minor & The Majors	(10)
5	15	I FOUND SOMEONE	Cher	(Geffen)
6	7	ANGEL EYES	Wet Wet Wet	(Precious Organisation)
7	21	COME INTO MY LIFE	Joyce Sims	(London)
8	2	FAIRYTALE	Pogues & Kirsty MacColl	(Pogue Mahone)
9	5	LOVE LETTERS	Alison Moyet	(CBS)
10	6	MY ARMS KEEP MISSING YOU	Rick Astley	(RCA)

WEEK 3

This Week	Last Week	Title	Artist	Label
1	1	HEAVEN IS A PLACE ON EARTH	Belinda Carlisle	(Virgin)
2	3	HOUSE ARREST	Krush	(Club)
3	14	SIGN YOUR NAME	Terence Trent D'Arby	(CBS)
4	4	STUTTER RAP	Morris Minor & The Majors	(10)
5	7	COME INTO MY LIFE	Joyce Sims	(London)
6	5	I FOUND SOMEONE	Cher	(Geffen)
7	42	I THINK WE'RE ALONE NOW	Tiffany	(MCA)
8	11	ALL DAY AND ALL OF THE NIGHT	Stranglers	(Epic)
9	19	RISE TO THE OCCASION	Climie Fisher	(EMI)
10	15	FATHER FIGURE	George Michael	(Epic)

WEEK 4

This Week	Last Week	Title	Artist	Label
1	7	I THINK WE'RE ALONE NOW	Tiffany	(MCA)
2	3	SIGN YOUR NAME	Terence Trent D'Arby	(CBS)
3	1	HEAVEN IS A PLACE ON EARTH	Belinda Carlisle	(Virgin)
4	2	HOUSE ARREST	Krush	(Club)
5	5	COME INTO MY LIFE	Joyce Sims	(London)
6	4	STUTTER RAP	Morris Minor & The Majors	(10)
7	30	WHEN WILL I BE FAMOUS	Bros	(CBS)
8	14	ROK DA HOUSE	Beatmasters featuring Cookie Crew	(Rhythm King)
9	9	RISE TO THE OCCASION	Climie Fisher	(EMI)
10	8	ALL DAY AND ALL OF THE NIGHT	Stranglers	(Epic)

TOP TEN ACT

KRUSH

It was clear from the start of 1988 that home-grown House and Hip-hop music was going to feature prominently in the Network Chart, and Krush quickly handcuffed the idea to the top ten with "House Arrest".

So many fads and fashions had emanated from London in the past, but this trio brought with their success not only a fresh sound but a new look - and it came from the provinces. Hailing from Sheffield and Nottingham, singer Ruthjoy and her friends Mark Gamble and Cassius Campbell were helped to their hit by a devoted clan of fans who called themselves Troopers.

They wore sports gear, baseball caps, leather jackets decorated with badges and motifs and were, Ruthjoy proudly pointed out, "just into dancing and wearing that gear."

Keeping up with the Trooper style was not without its minor problems, however. Just as followers of the Beastie Boys had copied the band's liking for wearing the Volkswagen car insignia by wantonly removing them from unattended vehicles, so Krush

fans would go in search of the Mercedes, Lamborghini and BMW motifs which their chosen group wore.

"The Trooper style comes from the Alphabet City part of New York, it's from the poor kids," Ruthjoy explained. "Cars are really big status symbols there, but they can't afford them so the next best thing is the insignia. Getting hold of one by taking it from someone else is not something we wish to encourage."

Just 20 years old at the time of "House Arrest", Ruthjoy had never sung a note before she recorded the single - and only agreed to do it then because she had been asked as a favour to Mark and Cassius. The favour certainly paid off - in addition to the song's British success, "House Arrest" reached the top ten in Germany, Holland, Switzerland and Israel. That was reason enough for Cassius to leave his previous employ to concentrate full time on music.

"The day we went into the charts, I quit my job in a pickle factory and never looked back," he grins.

Krush in a crush.

(RETNA)

FEBRUARY

NESCAFÉ · THE NETWORK CHART SHOW

NETWORK CHART TOP 40

1	1	*I THINK WE'RE ALONE NOW*	**Tiffany**	(MCA)
2	7	*WHEN WILL I BE FAMOUS*	**Bros**	(CBS)
3	2	*SIGN YOUR NAME*	**Terence Trent D'Arby**	(CBS)
4	3	*HEAVEN IS A PLACE ON EARTH*	**Belinda Carlisle**	(Virgin)
5	4	*HOUSE ARREST*	**Krush**	(Club)
6	8	*ROK DA HOUSE*	**Beatmasters featuring Cookie Crew**	(Rhythm King)
7	11	*OH L'AMOUR*	**Dollar**	(London)
8	5	*COME INTO MY LIFE*	**Joyce Sims**	(London)
9	9	*RISE TO THE OCCASION*	**Climie Fisher**	(EMI)
10	26	*SHAKE YOUR LOVE*	**Debbie Gibson**	(Atlantic)
11	29	*THE JACK THAT HOUSE BUILT*	**Jack 'N' Chill**	(10)
12	22	*CANDLE IN THE WIND*	**Elton John**	(Rocket)
13	18	*HOT IN THE CITY*	**Billy Idol**	(Chrysalis)
14	21	*TIRED*	**Two Guys, A Drum Machine & A Trumpet**	(London)
15	30	*TELL IT TO MY HEART*	**Taylor Dayne**	(Arista)
16	6	*STUTTER RAP*	**Morris Minor & The Majors**	(10)
17	42	*I SHOULD BE SO LUCKY*	**Kylie Minogue**	(PWL)
18	13	*IDEAL WORLD*	**The Christians**	(Island)
19	12	*HEAT SEEKER*	**AC/DC**	(Atlantic)
20	37	*VALENTINE*	**T'Pau**	(Siren)

Terence Trent D'Arby

(RETNA)

Debbie Gibson

(WEA)

21	34	*SAY IT AGAIN*	**Jermaine Stewart**	(10)
22	14	*I FOUND SOMEONE*	**Cher**	(Geffen)
23	16	*ANGEL EYES*	**Wet Wet Wet**	(Precious Organisation)
24	10	*ALL DAY AND ALL OF THE NIGHT*	**Stranglers**	(Epic)
25	35	*GIVE ME THE REASON*	**Luther Vandross**	(Epic)
26	17	*I CAN'T HELP IT*	**Bananarama**	(London)
27	20	*NEW SENSATION*	**INXS**	(Mercury)
28	41	*MANDINKA*	**Sinead O'Connor**	(Ensign)
29	46	*NO MORE LIES*	**Sharpe & Numan**	(Polydor)
30	15	*FATHER FIGURE*	**George Michael**	(Epic)
31	39	*I WANNA BE A FLINTSTONE*	**Screaming Blue Messiahs**	(WEA)
32	32	*WILD HEARTED WOMAN*	**All About Eve**	(Mercury)
33	25	*YOU'RE ALL I NEED*	**Motley Crue**	(Elektra)
34	19	*ALWAYS ON MY MIND*	**Pet Shop Boys**	(Parlophone)
35	38	*I GOT DA FEELIN'*	**Sweet Tee**	(Cooltempo)
36	56	*GIMME HOPE JO'ANNA*	**Eddy Grant**	(Ice)
37	23	*JINGO*	**Jellybean**	(Chrysalis)
38	60	*VICTORIA*	**Fall**	(Beggars Banquet)
39	40	*PROMISES*	**Basia**	(Epic)
40	NEW	*GIVE ME ALL YOUR LOVE*	**Whitesnake**	(EMI)

TIFFANY

All Tiffany Darwisch could think about when her debut single reached number one in America was... would she be spared the embarrassment of being applauded in front of her whole school at assembly?

At a time when most of her friends were raving about their favourite pop stars, she had suddenly become one herself - at the age of just 16!

Her version of "I Think We're Alone Now", a Sixties' smash for Tommy James and the Shondells, did not, however, have her hauled out in front of the school as she had feared - but it did lead to a long detention at the top of the Network Chart.

Musically, 1988 will be remembered for many reasons - the emergence of Bros and Acid House, to name but two - and it was a year in which a procession of teenage girl singers made their mark. But while contemporaries such as Debbie Gibson and Vanessa Paradis both enjoyed success, Tiffany was definitely top of the class. Unlike Debbie, she did not write any of her hits but proved she had the talent to sing them with style and conviction. Tiffany's talent was never in doubt, even before she was old enough to understand the meaning of the word. Born in Oklahoma on 2nd October, 1971, Tiffany's earliest memories are of singing.

"I began singing around the house when I was about two," she remembers, "but it wasn't until I reached nine years old that my parents took me seriously, and had me singing with Country and Western bands."

"Being a singer was my earliest ambition - that's all I ever thought about. From the time I was a little girl, I told my mum 'I'm going to be a singer when I grow up.'

"She would just laugh at me - she thought I'd want to be something else the next day - but I was determined to make this happen. Mind you, now that it actually HAS happened, I can hardly believe it."

When producer George Tobin first heard Tiffany singing in his studio, he could hardly believe it either! Having previously worked with the legendary soul performer Smokey Robinson, Tobin knew a star when he saw one and took over the musical guidance of his young discovery, eventually ending up as her manager. Within a month of him taking control of her career, she was signed to MCA Records - aged 14.

If the idea of a millionaire schoolgirl pop star seems a little strange, the way in which Tiffany promoted her first single is even weirder - The Shopping Mall Tour!

"MCA asked me to promote "I Think We're Alone Now" by appearing in hypermarkets all over America," explains Tiffany. "It sold a lot of records, and might have been even more profitable if I'd stopped spending so much of what I earned in clothes shops!"

Appropriately enough, Tiffany believes it's her image which has played a crucial part in her rise to fame.

"When I was a kid, I wanted to dress like my idols," she says, "so I wear clothes that other girls can copy. I did go through a phase of back-combing my hair and wearing tight black jeans, but it just wasn't me. Now, I simply wear what I feel happiest in - which is usully fairly casual clothes. I reckon that practically everyone in my audience owns a pair of jeans, a jumper and a T-shirt."

What they most certainly will not have is an international career to attend to at the same time as their homework, but Tiffany - who has now left school - reckons that if she could handle it, then almost anyone can.

Maybe she never quite got the hang of algebra, but she has learned enough about pop stardom to offer a few words of advice to those who long to follow her example.

"I'm doing everything I've always wanted to do," she says, "and if you have a chance to sing someplace - get up and do it. You never know who's going to be out there listening. Talent is one thing, but it's also about luck and who you know. That said, if you've got the slightest doubt about a singing career, then aim for something less risky - like hang-gliding. But deep down in your heart, if you're sure it's waht you want to do... go for it!"

Tiffany – star of stage, screen and shopping centres!

FEBRUARY

NUMBER

1

ONE ACT

WHO'S BAD?

As all self-respecting trendy types will doubtlessly be aware, bad can also mean good - but when it comes to Michael Jackson, many music fans think "Bad" is positively the worst.

In a poll published during February in the influential American rock magazine Rolling Stone, 23,000 readers voted Jackson bottom in no less that eight categories - the same total of Grammys he was awarded for "Bad's" predecessor, "Thriller".

Among other 'victories', the world's most phenomenal peformer was judged by the survey to be the worst singer and the worst dressed, while "Bad" and its title track were condemned as the worst album and the worst single. All of which, according to the journal's music editor, David Wild, had more to do with the singer's rather odd personality and behaviour than any real criticism of his enormously popular music.

"People were responding negatively to his image and to the hype," he explained. "The category he should have won is 'worst image', or 'least understood'."

Not that Jackson will have been too concerned about the uncomplimentary results as they stood. He can afford to smile as "Bad" is approaching sales of 20 million worldwide ("Thriller" has already topped 40 million copies to become the biggest-selling album of all time). He can afford to chuckle about it reaching number one in 25 countries - from Argentina to Austria, from Holland to Hong Kong - and he may even shed a tear of joy about the string of hit singles it provided him with!

True, Jackson will have been disappointed that his efforts this time around earned him only one award at the 1988 Grammys - for best engineering - but any sadness he might have felt will have been quickly erased by the staggering success of his debut solo world tour.

It began in Japan on September 10, 1987, and by the time it reached Britain in July the following year, he had peformed to more than five million people - all prepared to vote for him. Now that's not BAD

Michael Jackson steps forward to accept the "Worst Jacket In The World" award.

(RETNA)

HE WHO LANDS LAST

At the 1988 Olympics, a humble 24-year-old plasterer from Cheltenham gave a whole new meaning to that most British of sporting ideals - it's not the winning but the taking part which counts!

For a few brief moments out there in Calgary during February, Eddie 'The Eagle' Edwards actually made losing a far more spectacular and successful feat than any victory and, as Britain's lone representative in the ski-jumping event, he could not have lost more convincingly. Competing in both the 70 and 90 metre ski-jump disciplines of what is recognised as the most dangerous Olympic event, Eddie proudly came in 58th and 55th. (There were no 59th and 56th entrants!)

Triumphant in defeat, he became the star of the Games - outshining even the real and momentous achievements of Britain's true heroes like short-track speed skater Wilf O'Reilly, who broke world records on his way to two gold medals, and downhill skier Martin Bell, whose eighth place in one race was the best ever finish by a Briton. Even the all-conquering superstars of the Olympics, like skater Katarina Witt or skier Pirmin Zurbriggen, were beaten into oblivion by the amount of media attention lowly Eddie attracted. His mere attendance, sighed the Americans, "symbolised the spirit of the Olympics; just taking part against all the odds." Others took a less lofty view of the mad daredevil hurling himself into space with absolutely no chance of winning. "We have a thousand like Eddie at home in Norway," shrugged one Scandinavian. "We just don't let them compete..."

However he was considered, Eddie - who took up ski-jumping "because I'd seem some blokes doing it on TV and liked the look of it" - became an international celebrity overnight. He appeared alongside actor Burt Reynolds on the famous Johnny Carson Show in America, was greeted by 10,000 of his townfolk on his glorious return to Cheltenham, and is even now preparing for the 1992 Winter Olympics in France, seriously hoping for a medal.

Naturally, some say Eddie is bonkers, but he's heard that one before. "It's not that I'm mad," he offers, "it's just that I don't decide something is impossible until I've thought about it. If you asked me to jump off a 3,000 ft cliff with no parachute, I wouldn't say no. I'd go away and think about it..."

Eddie the Eagle checks the crosswind with his tongue.

Vreni Schneider displays the style that brought her gold in the women's slalom and giant slalom.

(ALLSPORT)

(ALLSPORT)

TOP 10 MUSIC VIDEOS

This Week	Last Week	Title	Artist	Label
1	1	CV	Peter Gabriel	(Virgin)
2	3	LIVE	Eurythmics	(Polygram)
3	4	LIVE UNDER A BLOOD RED SKY	U2	(Channel 5)
4	2	SLIPPERY WHEN WET	Bon Jovi	(Channel 5)
6	15	THE BEST OF UB40	UB40	(Virgin)
7	39	VISIBLE TOUCH	Genesis	(Virgin)
8	48	FAMILY OF FIVE	Level 42	(Channel 5)
9	21	OLIVE	Prince & The Revolution	(Paisley Park)
10	16	MAGIC YEARS VOLUME 1	Queen	(PMI)

TOP 20 ALBUMS

This Week	Last Week	Title	Artist	Label
1	2	THE HARDLINE ACCORDING TO...	Terence Trent D'Arby	(CBS)
2	4	IF I SHOULD FALL FROM GRACE	Pogues	(Pogue Mahone)
3	1	TURN BACK THE CLOCK	Johnny Hates Jazz	(Virgin)
4	5	THE CHRISTIANS	The Christians	(Chrysalis)
5	3	POPPED IN SOULED OUT	Wet Wet Wet	(Precious Organisation)
6	6	HEAVEN ON EARTH	Belinda Carlisle	(Virgin)
7	7	BAD	Michael Jackson	(Epic)
8	10	COME INTO MY LIFE	Joyce Sims	(London)
9	15	TANGO IN THE NIGHT	Fleetwood Mac	(Warner Brothers)
10	14	JACK MIX '86-'88	Mirage	(Stylus)
11	11	BRIDGE OF SPIES	T'Pau	(Siren)
12	8	FAITH	George Michael	(Epic)
13	13	KICK	INXS	(Mercury)
14	NEW	SKYSCRAPER	David Lee Roth	(Warner Brothers)
15	9	WHENEVER YOU NEED SOMEBODY	Rick Astley	(RCA)
16	16	ACTUALLY	Pet Shop Boys	(Parlophone)
17	18	RAINDANCING	Alison Moyet	(CBS)
18	12	LIFE IN THE FAST LANE	Various	(Telstar)
19	20	WHITNEY	Whitney Houston	(Arista)
20	24	WHITESNAKE 1987	Whitesnake	(EMI)

TOP 10 SINGLES

WEEK 2

This Week	Last Week	Title	Artist	Label
1	1	I THINK WE'RE ALONE NOW	Tiffany	(MCA)
2	2	WHEN WILL I BE FAMOUS	Bros	(CBS)
3	15	TELL IT TO MY HEART	Taylor Dayne	(Arista)
4	17	I SHOULD BE SO LUCKY	Kylie Minogue	(PWL)
5	6	ROK DA HOUSE	Beatmasters featuring Cookie Crew	(Rhythm King)
6	10	SHAKE YOUR LOVE	Debbie Gibson	(Atlantic)
7	7	OH L'AMOUR	Dollar	(London)
8	11	THE JACK THAT HOUSE BUILT	Jack 'N' Chill	(10)
9	3	SIGN YOUR NAME	Terence Trent D'Arby	(CBS)
10	12	CANDLE IN THE WIND	Elton John	(Rocket)

WEEK 3

This Week	Last Week	Title	Artist	Label
1	4	I SHOULD BE SO LUCKY	Kylie Minogue	(PWL)
2	1	I THINK WE'RE ALONE NOW	Tiffany	(MCA)
3	3	TELL IT TO MY HEART	Taylor Dayne	(Arista)
4	17	GET OUT OF MY DREAMS	Billy Ocean	(Jive)
5	2	WHEN WILL I BE FAMOUS	Bros	(CBS)
6	10	CANDLE IN THE WIND	Elton John	(Rocket)
7	6	SHAKE YOUR LOVE	Debbie Gibson	(Atlantic)
8	8	THE JACK THAT HOUSE BUILT	Jack 'N' Chill	(10)
9	15	SAY IT AGAIN	Jermaine Stewart	(10)
10	13	VALENTINE	T'Pau	(Siren)

WEEK 4

This Week	Last Week	Title	Artist	Label
1	1	I SHOULD BE SO LUCKY	Kylie Minogue	(PWL)
2	19	BEAT DIS	Bomb The Bass	(Rhythm King)
3	4	GET OUT OF MY DREAMS	Billy Ocean	(Jive)
4	3	TELL IT TO MY HEART	Taylor Dayne	(Arista)
5	2	I THINK WE'RE ALONE NOW	Tiffany	(MCA)
6	9	SAY IT AGAIN	Jermaine Stewart	(10)
7	10	VALENTINE	T'Pau	(Siren)
8	20	GIMME HOPE JO'ANNA	Eddy Grant	(Ice)
9	6	CANDLE IN THE WIND	Elton John	(Rocket)
10	5	WHEN WILL I BE FAMOUS	Bros	(CBS)

TOP TEN ACT
T'PAU

(RETNA)

It was doubly appropriate that T'Pau should make the Network Chart Top Ten in February.

Firstly, the hit which put them there in the week of St. Valentine's Day was called..."Valentine", and secondly, the very success of the group has been borne out of good, old-fashioned romance.

Singer Carol Decker and rhythm guitarist Ronnie Rogers have been together for seven years - long before, Carol points out, T'Pau was anything more than the name of a Vulcan priestess in Star Trek. "We're simply in the same band, we're in love - and that's just the way it worked out," she says.

The pair met one night at a Shropshire pub called The Star, where Ronnie was performing with a band called The Katz and Carol, then singing with The Lazers, was among the audience. More impressed by his looks than his playing - "It was lust at first sight!" she laughs - Carol wasted little time in asking Ronnie to join her group.

Happy though they were together, the music scene in and around Shrewsbury was not exactly brimming with possibilities.

"Everybody in Shropshire has got good intentions and big, big pipe dreams," Carol considers, "but no idea of how to organise anything - and there's nowhere for people to play. The discos took over and they killed live music."

So, after playing as many farmers' hoe-downs and working men's clubs locally as they could suffer, Carol and Ronnie left The Lazers in 1984, scraped together some money to buy a four-track tape recorder and began writing songs in their rented Shrewsbury flat. T'Pau formed in the spring of 1986 and, later that year, the band's debut single began climbing the American charts, finally settling at number four.

"Heart and Soul", a song which the Nolans were offered, eventually achieved the same placing in Britain and was followed by one of the biggest hits of 1987 - "China In Your Hand ".

Since then, T'Pau has gone on to establish a faithful following with sell-out tours and two hit albums, but Carol hasn't forgotten the hopeless times when love was all she had.

"We've waited a long time for our success," she says, "and we were penniless for ages before it happened. But at least Ronnie and me were broke together!"

Carol Decker practises touching her nose with her tongue ...

(RETNA)

... and has a laugh with the lads.

THE NETWORK CHART SHOW

NETWORK CHART TOP 40

(ARISTA)

Taylor Dane

Mel and Kim

(RETNA)

1	1	*I SHOULD BE SO LUCKY*	Kylie Minogue	(PWL)
2	2	*BEAT DIS*	Bomb The Bass	(Rhythm King)
3	3	*GET OUT OF MY DREAMS*	Billy Ocean	(Jive)
4	13	*SUEDEHEAD*	Morrissey	(HMV)
5	20	*TOGETHER FOREVER*	Rick Astley	(RCA)
6	4	*TELL IT TO MY HEART*	Taylor Dayne	(Arista)
7	8	*GIMME HOPE JO'ANNA*	Eddy Grant	(Ice)
8	16	*DOCTORIN' THE HOUSE*	Cold Cut	(Ahead Of Our Time)
9	17	*JOE LE TAXI*	Vanessa Paradis	(FA Productions)
10	5	*I THINK WE'RE ALONE NOW*	Tiffany	(MCA)
11	6	*SAY IT AGAIN*	Jermaine Stewart	(10)
12	12	*MAN IN THE MIRROR*	Michael Jackson	(Epic)
13	34	*THAT'S THE WAY IT IS*	Mel & Kim	(Supreme)
14	29	*DOMINION*	Sisters of Mercy	(Merciful Release)
15	25	*HAZY SHADE OF WINTER*	Bangles	(Def Jam)
16	11	*TOWER OF STRENGTH*	Mission	(Mercury)
17	36	*CRASH*	Primitives	(RCA)
18	31	*C'MON EVERYBODY*	Eddie Cochran	(Liberty)
19	9	*CANDLE IN THE WIND*	Elton John	(Rocket)
20	7	*VALENTINE*	T'Pau	(Siren)
21	10	*WHEN WILL I BE FAMOUS*	Bros	(CBS)
22	24	*NEVER KNEW LOVE*	Alexander O'Neal/Cherrelle	(Tabu)
23	73	*GOODGROOVE*	Derek B	(Music Of Life)
24	33	*WHEN WE WAS FAB*	George Harrison	(Dark Horse)
25	15	*SPY IN THE HOUSE OF LOVE*	Was (Not Was)	(Fontana)
26	61	*I GET WEAK*	Belinda Carlisle	(Virgin)
27	14	*SHAKE YOUR LOVE*	Debbie Gibson	(Atlantic)
28	44	*HEART OF GOLD*	Johnny Hates Jazz	(Virgin)
29	28	*I DON'T MIND AT ALL*	Bourgeois Tagg	(Island)
30	67	*LOVE IS CONTAGIOUS*	Taja Sevelle	(Paisley Park)
31	39	*PEOPLE ARE STRANGE*	Echo & The Bunnymen	(WEA)
32	18	*THE JACK THAT HOUSE BUILT*	Jack 'N' Chill	(10)
33	21	*MANDINKA*	Sinead O'Connor	(Ensign)
34	19	*ROK DA HOUSE*	Beatmasters featuring Cookie Crew	(Rhythm King)
35	35	*GOING TO CALI/JACK THE RIPPER*	L.L. Cool J	(Def Jam)
36	30	*DIGNITY*	Deacon Blue	(CBS)
37	47	*HOW MEN ARE*	Aztec Camera	(WEA)
38	55	*I'M NOT SCARED*	Eighth Wonder	(CBS)
39	NEW	*SHIP OF FOOLS*	Erasure	(Mute)
40	23	*LET'S GET BRUTAL*	Nitro Deluxe	(Cooltempo)

KYLIE MINOGUE

There are pop stars who believe they can act, and actors who imagine they can sing, but there are very few who are actually good at both.

Kylie Minogue chose 1988 to prove quite emphatically that she is definitely amongst the multi-talented ones. Yet the tiny 20-year-old from Melbourne, Australia, might simply have settled for the fame she had won playing Charlene in Neighbours were it not for the 'accident' which launched her career as a singer.

During a benefit concert at an Australian rules football club in July 1987, the cast of the soap opera joined the ranks to sing and raise money.

"We ended up singing 'Locomotion' - which was the only song I knew all the words to," Kylie recalls, "and it all just seemed to snowball from there."

Impressed by her sweet voice, a representative from Mushroom Records swiftly whisked Kylie into a studio to record the song, and the following month it reached number one in Australia - and stayed put for seven weeks! The impact she made did not escape Stock, Aitken and Waterman and, in September, they invited Kylie over to London for ten days to record some more songs, several specially written for her.

Among them was "I Should Be So Lucky" which became a Network Chart number one at the same time that Neighbours mania gripped Britain - with the series attracting chart-topping status itself in the TV ratings.

"It was amazing," says Kylie. "I mean, I never had any aspirations to be a pop star - except that, when I was about eight or nine, I used to have pretend Abba concerts in my bedroom with my friends. We'd put on dresses, dance to Abba records and pretend to be the group. We'd prance about the bedroom or the lounge, singing into hairbrushes, but that's about as far as my pop singing ambitions went.

"Mind you, I've always felt very confident about singing, and acting is such a dicey profession that I wanted something else."

Not that Kylie has ever been short of work - she has been successful and in demand for more than half her life.

"The first thing I did was when I was ten years old and I appeared in one episode of a TV show called Skyways. Oddly enough, I was in that with Jason Donovan - it was his first job too - but that didn't last very long because it was pretty dreadful."

It was good enough for Kylie to make a favourable impression, however, and a year later she found herself playing the part of a Dutch girl called Carla in the popular Australian soap opera The Sullivans. Kylie joined Neighbours straight after completing her Higher School Certificate - the Australian equivalent of GCSEs - and immediately had to cope with a 12-hour working day.

"Normally, I'd get up at 6am, get to the studio at 7am - and not finish until 7pm. then I'd get home and have to do loads of interviews, and on top of that I'd have to learn my lines."

The added demands of her successful singing career eventually meant that something had to go and, for the moment, Kylie has decided it should be acting. She left Neighbours in June (1988).

"I'd worked on the show for two-and-a-half years, and the cast and crew had really become like a family," she says. "I cried and cried at the farewell party they gave for me, but the best thing about leaving is that I wasn't actually killed off when I filmed my final scenes. The producers have told me that the door's open any time I want to climb back into Charlene's clothes again."

The offer is one Kylie greatly appreciates because, for all her success, she knows it could all end as quickly as it began.

"I can't stop wondering why it's me that's had all the luck," she explains. "Sometimes I think about all the people out there breaking their necks to become actresses or singers, and I feel sure my luck won't last. It's true, in a couple of months' times, I could be a nobody."

She should be so unlucky...

Kylie used to pretend she was in Abba!

(RETNA)

HAPPY BIRTHDAY SUPERMAN

They were two shy, awkward kids with a multi-million dollar idea that nobody wanted. For five disheartening years, Jerry Siegel and Joe Schuster faced rejection at every turn.

A pair of unlikely lads from Cleveland, Ohio, they were laughed out of town along with the cartoon character they had created - and heard at least one smug newspaper editor call their invention "too preposterous for words."

Finally, they got a long-awaited break when a new publication agreed to carry their strip - even putting its hero on the cover - and when Volume One, Number One of Action Comics hit the street in June, 1938, Superman was born.

In 1988, the Man of Steel celebrated his fiftieth birthday. His precise date of arrival on earth is in some doubt, but the June issue of Action Comics was available in March. In any case, his half-decade of heart-stopping existence has captured the world's imagination and transformed him into the ultimate crime-busting hero.

It has also seen his adventures leap from the pages of a comic into more than 250 newspapers, through 13 years of radio shows, three novels, 17 animated cartoons, two movie serials of 15 instalments each, a TV series of 104 episodes, a second animated cartoon series of 69 parts, a Broadway musical and five blockbusting films with a sixth in the making.

The idea for Superman came to Siegel one night as he lay counting sheep in bed.

"I'd conceived a character like Samson, Hercules and all the strong men I'd ever heard of rolled into one - only more so," he reveals. Of course, the hero's deeds had to be equally magnificent, and as the years have rolled by, so the powers of Superman - alias the wimpish Daily Planet reporter Clark Kent - have progressed.

Not only can he leap tall buildings in a single bound, outrun a locomotive or penetrate a wall with his X-ray vision, but he can also circle the globe at superspeed in 90 seconds, catch a crashing helicopter and solder San Francisco's Golden Gate Bridge together.

Each of his fantastic, fearless feats are outrageous and unbelievable enough to ensure that the millions of fans who follow his amazing exploits in 15 languages and 30 countries will still be cheering Superman when he reaches his 100th birthday.

(REX FEATURES)

Christopher Reeve as the Man of Steel in Superman – The Movie.

THE ICE QUEEN

Budapest, March 27, 1988 - a place and time that will go down in sporting history as the end of a golden era.

It was the location which provided the setting for the World Figure Skating Championships, and the date which not only saw the final day of proceedings but also the retirement of East Germany's Katarina Witt. One of the sport's all-time great stars, she waved auf wiedersehen to competition - with yet another ladies' individual gold medal in her pocket.

At the age of just 23, she might have seemed too young to hang up her boots, but after 17 years of training and tournaments she slid gracefully out with a most staggering collection of victories; six consecutive European titles, two Olympic gold medals - at Sarajevo in 1984 and Calgary in 1988 - and a fourth World crown to add to her previous triumphs in 1984, 1985 and 1987.

Born in Karl Marx Stadt, Katarina took up skating at the tender age of five - and even at kindergarten she was already pestering her parents to let her improve her skills with lessons in the sport. When they eventually gave in to her pressure and agreed, it didn't take long before her potential as a future champion was shining through. When she was nine years old she started training with the top East German coach Jutta Muller, but no amount of practice or tuition was responsible for giving Katarina that extra edge which would so often set her apart from her frustrated, also-ran rivals.

Her natural skating abilities aside, Katarina was always widely praised for her beauty - her admirers include Michael Jackson - as well as for her shapely figure and revealing outfits. Her dress style often landed her in hot water with fellow competitors and skating officials alike, but Katarina shrugged off any such criticism with a smile.

"When I wear the right costume, I feel much better," she explained, "and why not stress what we have that is attractive?"

Now skating professionally and pursuing a career as an actress, the offers of work which have flooded in since her last championship are proof that what Katarina wants to stress is what people want to see...

(ALLSPORT)

Katarina Witt falls asleep on one leg.

TOP 10 MUSIC VIDEOS

THIS WEEK	LAST WEEK	Title	Artist	Label
1	1	CV	Peter Gabriel	(Virgin)
2	2	MORE VITAL IDOL	Billy Idol	(Chrysalis)
3	3	THE VOICE ON VIDEO	Alexander O'Neal	(CBS/Fox)
4	7	SLIPPERY WHEN WET	Bon Jovi	(Channel 5)
5	4	LIVE UNDER A BLOOD RED SKY	U2	(Virgin)
6	6	VISIBLE TOUCH	Genesis	(Virgin)
7	5	LIVE	Eurythmics	(Polygram)
8	8	MAGIC YEARS VOLUME 1	Queen	(PMI)
9	10	THE BEST OF UB40	UB40	(Virgin)
10	14	MAGIC YEARS VOLUME 2	Queen	(PMI)

TOP 20 ALBUMS

THIS WEEK	LAST WEEK	Title	Artist	Label
1	1	THE HARDLINE ACCORDING TO	Terence Trent D'Arby	(CBS)
2	4	THE CHRISTIANS	The Christians	(Chrysalis)
3	6	POPPED IN SOULED OUT	Wet Wet Wet	(Precious Organisation)
4	2	BRIDGE OF SPIES	T'Pau	(Siren)
5	17	ALL ABOUT EVE	All About Eve	(Mercury)
6	7	WHENEVER YOU NEED SOMEBODY	Rick Astley	(RCA)
7	5	TURN BACK THE CLOCK	Johnny Hates Jazz	(Virgin)
8	13	BAD	Michael Jackson	(Epic)
9	23	TIFFANY	Tiffany	(MCA)
10	3	ACTUALLY	Pet Shop Boys	(Parlophone)
11	15	TANGO IN THE NIGHT	Fleetwood Mac	(Warner Brothers)
12	8	COME INTO MY LIFE	Joyce Sims	(London)
13	9	FAITH	George Michael	(Epic)
14	16	NOTHING LIKE THE SUN	Sting	(A&M)
15	18	THE SILVER COLLECTION	Dusty Springfield	(Phillips)
16	20	GIVE ME THE REASON	Luther Vandross	(Epic)
17	19	THE JOSHUA TREE	U2	(Island)
18	24	HEARSAY	Alexander O'Neal	(Tabu)
19	25	HEAVEN ON EARTH	Belinda Carlisle	(Virgin)
20	10	GREATEST LOVE	Various	(Telstar)

TOP 10 SINGLES

WEEK 2

THIS WEEK	LAST WEEK	Title	Artist	Label
1	1	I SHOULD BE SO LUCKY	Kylie Minogue	(PWL)
2	2	BEAT DIS	Bomb The Bass	(Rhythm King)
3	5	TOGETHER FOREVER	Rick Astley	(RCA)
4	9	JOE LE TAXI	Vanessa Paradis	(FA Productions)
5	3	GET OUT OF MY DREAMS	Billy Ocean	(Jive)
6	4	SUEDEHEAD	Morrissey	(HMV)
7	8	DOCTORIN' THE HOUSE	Cold Cut	(Ahead Of Our Time)
8	26	I GET WEAK	Belinda Carlisle	(Virgin)
9	17	CRASH	Primitives	(RCA)
10	15	HAZY SHADE OF WINTER	Bangles	(Def Jam)

WEEK 3

THIS WEEK	LAST WEEK	Title	Artist	Label
1	1	I SHOULD BE SO LUCKY	Kylie Minogue	(PWL)
2	3	TOGETHER FOREVER	Rick Astley	(RCA)
3	4	JOE LE TAXI	Vanessa Paradis	(FA Productions)
4	2	BEAT DIS	Bomb The Bass	(Rhythm King)
5	7	DOCTORIN' THE HOUSE	Cold Cut	(Ahead Of Our Time)
6	9	CRASH	Primitives	(RCA)
7	8	I GET WEAK	Belinda Carlisle	(Virgin)
8	16	SHIP OF FOOLS	Erasure	(Mute)
9	21	NEVER/THESE DREAMS	Heart	(Capitol)
10	18	LOVE IS CONTAGIOUS	Taja Sevelle	(Paisley Park)

WEEK 4

THIS WEEK	LAST WEEK	Title	Artist	Label
1	14	DON'T TURN AROUND	Aswad	(Mango)
2	1	I SHOULD BE SO LUCKY	Kylie Minogue	(PWL)
3	2	TOGETHER FOREVER	Rick Astley	(RCA)
4	10	LOVE IS CONTAGIOUS	Taja Sevelle	(Paisley Park)
5	8	SHIP OF FOOLS	Erasure	(Mute)
6	3	JOE LE TAXI	Vanessa Paradis	(FA Productions)
7	6	CRASH	Primitives	(RCA)
8	9	NEVER/THESE DREAMS	Heart	(Capitol)
9	34	DROP THE BOY	Bros	(CBS)
10	19	WHERE DO BROKEN HEARTS GO?	Whitney Houston	(Arista)

TOP TEN ACT
THE PRIMITIVES

Depending on the story she chooses to tell, Tracey Tracey joined The Primitives in a variety of different ways and on several different occasions.

One version suggests it happened after she was approached on top of a double-decker bus by a strange youth. He said "We've heard you sing - wanna join our band?" But the most consistent tale of how she came to be in the band involves nothing more original than responding to an advert she came across in her local library.

Whatever the case might really be, the mysterious 'arrivals' of Tracey within The Primitives fits in perfectly with the music they make.

"I like to look at our songs as little holidays from life," says bass player Sensitive Steve. "Nobody could ever gain any kind of inspiration from our lyrics, we'll never change anyone's life... so we try to thrill 'em. Make 'em happy."

Most would agree that The Primitives' debut Network Chart top ten hit in March succeeded in doing that, but it was not always simply a matter of fun for the Coventry group.

"When we first started, we were just a noise," Steve admits. "We were a real thrash. That's still important to us, but now we want sweet melodies, nice catchy pop tunes - and they've got to have noise as well."

Until The Primitives came thrashing noisily along, the most celebrated musical exports from their hometown had been The Specials and King, and the national success of local Coventry talent might have ended there if Tracey had taken a shine to Kylie's country.

"My parents emigrated to Australia a few years ago," she explains, "and it's possible to do really well there. You can have a massive house, a swimming pool and lead a life of luxury. I got tired of it, so I moved back to Coventry to be in a group."

Having achieved the ambition of joining a band, Tracey - like the rest of The Primitives - finds herself bewildered by the impact of a hit single - albeit one called "Crash".

"People suddenly expect you to have all the answers to the world's problems," says Steve. "I can't even sort out my own"!"

The Primitives shelter in a darkened room after having too much sun.

(RETNA)

(RETNA)

NETWORK CHART TOP 40

1	1	DON'T TURN AROUND	**Aswad**	(Mango)
2	9	DROP THE BOY	**Bros**	(CBS)
3	14	COULD'VE BEEN	**Tiffany**	(MCA)
4	26	CAN'T PLAY WITH MADNESS	**Iron Maiden**	(EMI)
5	2	I SHOULD BE SO LUCKY	**Kylie Minogue**	(PWL)
6	8	NEVER/THESE DREAMS	**Heart**	(Capital)
7	23	CROSS MY BROKEN HEART	**Sinitta**	(Fanfare)
8	36	STAY ON THESE ROADS	**A-Ha**	(Warner Brothers)
9	16	I'M NOT SCARED	**Eighth Wonder**	(CBS)
10	10	WHERE DO BROKEN HEARTS GO?	**Whitney Houston**	(Arista)
11	19	BASS (HOW LOW CAN YOU GO)	**Simon Harris**	(london)
12	6	JOE LE TAXI	**Vanessa Paradis**	(FA Productions)
13	25	ONLY IN MY DREAMS	**Debbie Gibson**	(Atlantic)
14	13	I GET WEAK	**Belinda Carlisle**	(Virgin)
15	NEW	HEART	**Pet Shop Boys**	(Parlophone)
16	5	SHIP OF FOOLS	**Erasure**	(Mute)
17	4	LOVE IS CONTAGIOUS	**Taja Sevelle**	(Paisley Park)
18	20	TEMPTATION	**Wet Wet Wet**	(Precious Organisation)
19	3	TOGETHER FOREVER	**Rick Astley**	(RCA)
20	7	CRASH	**Primitives**	(RCA)
21	17	RECKLESS	**Afrika Bambaataa & UB40**	(EMI)
22	24	I WANT HER	**Keith Sweat**	(Elektra)
23	32	LOVE CHANGES EVERYTHING	**Climie Fisher**	(EMI)
24	11	I KNOW YOU GOT SOUL	**Eric B. & Rakim**	(Cooltempo)
25	15	DOCTORIN' THE HOUSE	**Cold Cut**	(Ahead Of Our Time)
26	12	BEAT DIS	**Bomb The Bass**	(Mister Ron)
27	29	DREAMING	**Glen Goldsmith**	(RCA)
28	18	HEART OF GOLD	**Johnny Hates Jazz**	(Virgin)
29	33	PROVE YOUR LOVE	**Taylor Dayne**	(Arista)
30	55	AIN'T COMPLAINING	**Status Quo**	(Vertigo)
31	34	I FOUGHT THE LAW	**Clash**	(CBS)
32	NEW	THAT'S THE WAY I WANNA ROCK 'N' ROLL	**AC/DC**	(Atlantic)
33	31	DAYS OF NO TRUST	**Magnum**	(Polydor)
34	44	GIRLFRIEND	**Pebbles**	(MCA)
35	21	GET OUT OF MY DREAMS	**Billy Ocean**	(Jive)
36	45	JUST A MIRAGE	**Jellybean**	(Chrysalis)
37	27	THAT'S THE WAY IT IS	**Mel & Kim**	(Supreme)
38	38	I PRONOUNCE YOU	**The Madness**	(Virgin)
39	66	PINK CADILLAC	**Natalie Cole**	(Manhattan)
40	NEW	LOVE IS STRONGER THAN PRIDE	**Sade**	(Epic)

(RETNA)

Bomb the Bass – time to give up smoking!

Eighth Wonder under a sun lamp with all their clothes on.

(CBS)

A S W A D

NUMBER ① ONE ACT

Of all the hits in 1988, none took a longer time coming that "Don't Turn Around".

Not only did it provide Aswad with a debut number one on the Network Chart, but also achieved the group's first Top 40 hit in a career stretching back no less than 14 years!

"The highest position we'd ever reached before was 41," says drummer Angus 'Drummie Zeb' Gaye, "but we've never given up what we believe in. We've stuck together."

Indeed, the relentless quest for chart celebrity has always been the furthest notion in the ambitions of Aswad. Instead, the group set out with the aim of spreading the music and message of reggae, but in a peculiarly British way. For that very reason, Aswad quickly became known as 'The Young Lions of British Reggae' after forming in London's Ladbroke Grove area during 1974.

"It makes us sound old, but we were taking school exams when we made our first album," explains singer Brinsley Forde, who founded the group with Drummie and later recruited his old school friend Tony Gad to play bass guitar. The trio's early days together were not without lean times.

"It was hard in the beginning," Tony admits, "and me and Brinsley had to live in squats. I did actually get a flat in Ladbroke Grove, but I had no money and the bailiffs came and turfed me out. It was very rough but, the thing is, all we were bothered about was that our music was good and that we were enjoying it. It was only later that we realised if we were going to make any money, then we'd have to take a more business-like approach."

From the start, however, Aswad could boast a faithful following to match their commitment about taking reggae to a wider audience. The group's records might not have sold in any great quantities, but Aswad concerts never failed to earn them a 'Sold Out' sign by the door.

Prior to the success of "Don't Turn Around", Aswad played to a full house at London's Hammersmith Odeon in the first reggae concert to be held at the venue since a show by the late Bob Marley eight years previously.

"We took that as a sure sign that reggae music is growing," says Brinsley, "and what a lot of people need to realise is that our fans have always been multi-racial, always been across the board."

That Aswad have survived this far down the road is a testament to that appeal - countless other reggae bands have fallen by the wayside in the meantime.

"In the early Seventies, there were a lot of them coming through," Drummie considers, "but we wanted to make reggae music that identified with Britain, because we live here and, as far as we are concerned, that spirit of reggae will never die. Reggae is rarely written for chart success alone. The lyrics deal with reality, there's no compromise."

Yet that is precisely what Aswad - the name means 'black' in the Arabic language - was accused of doing in order to finally secure a hit with "Don't Turn Around". Far more obviously commercial than many previous releases by the group, it was not even self-penned. Originally intended for Tina Turner, the song was written by Albert Hammond and Diane Warren - the partnership responsible for the second biggest-selling single of 1987 - Starship's "Nothing's Going To Stop Us Now". Aswad say that they could see the shouts of 'sell out' coming.

"Our music hasn't changed," Drummie shrugs. "We've always progressed and made different kinds of music. Just because we've been successful, it doesn't mean that people should say 'They've sold out' or 'It's not hip to like Aswad any more.' Just because we've had some hits now, it doesn't mean that our music is any less good."

Brinsley, who does his best to play down a career as a young actor in which the highlight was a role as Brains in the BBC children's series The Doubledeckers, is even more protective of the 'sudden' arrival of Aswad as a household name.

"It's not Aswad who have changed," he reasons, "it's people..."

(RETNA)

Aswad making music on a deserted tropical brick wall.

EMPEROR OSCAR

The unprecedented success of The Last Emperor at the 60th Academy awards was a glittering triumph for the movie that almost never was, and a piece of pure Hollywood.

(RETNA)

For, in a saga worthy of a film script itself, the true-life epic of Aisin Gioro Pu Yi - China's final feudal ruler - picked up nine Oscars, having originally been turned down by every major film studio. Warner Bros, 20th Century Fox, Columbia... all of the large film-making corporations passed on the opportunity to help finance the project. For four years, British producer Jeremy Thomas touted the idea around Hollywood, finally securing most of the $23.8 million required from banks - and even sinking in $200,000 of his own. It was a gamble worth taking; the film is now expected to earn $140 million worldwide.

But the cost of getting The Last Emperor off the ground - and its budget was less than many more modest-looking films - was almost a minor problem compared with the logistics of actually filming it. Permission was granted to shoot scenes in Beijing's Forbidden City (where the emperor had grown up a pampered prisoner), after negotiations by director Bernardo Bertolucci in 1984.

"I got to film in courtyards of the Forbidden City that had not been opened in 50 years," he says. "On the first day, an old guard unlocked doors with rusty keys not used in decades. It was incredible."

So, too, was the sheer size of the cast during filming the child emperor's coronation.

"I had 3,000 extras for three days," Bertolucci recalls, "and all I remember is these military trucks vomiting thousands of people. I completely panicked. I wanted to shut myself up in hospital!"

He also won the Oscar for Best Director to go with the Last Emperor's other awards; Best Picture, Best Art Direction, Best Cinematography, Best Sound, Best Original Score, Best Screenplay Adaptation, Best Costumes and Best Film Editing.

Cher and Michael Douglas – Best Actress and Best Actor.

RUNNING ALL OVER THE WORLD

Around the world, more than 15 million children die needlessly each year from hunger, poverty and disease. Two more just died in the time it took to read that sentence...

It was with such horrifying statistics in mind that Sport Aid '88 was officially launched in April, in a bid to do something about so many wasted young lives. Following on from the 1986 Sport Aid activities - which themselves stemmed from the massive Live Aid concert - the fund-raising kicked off with a series of sponsored 1,000-metre races for children around the globe, and would culminate several months later in the biggest mass participation event in history.

That came on Sunday, September 11, when at precisely 1500 hours Greenwich Mean Time - 4pm in Britain - an estimated 50 million people in 128 countries took part in the 'Race Against Time'. It was a sporting feat which the Pope was moved to describe as "a race for goodness" and it witnessed runners across five continents simultaneously stepping out to help those less fortunate.

The original Sport Aid had raised £24 million after 20 million people in 89 countries ran for charity at a similar event, and the 1988 race easily topped those figures. In Britain, runners took part in almost 200 cities and towns - and in Hyde Park, London, around 50,000 turned up for the 10-kilometre fun run.

Of the money raised in developed countries, 20 per cent will be retained to help local youngsters, while the remainder goes to such international organisations as Care and Unicef. Poorer nations kept all the cash they raised.

However, the point of Sport Aid '88 was not simply to find cash, but also to increase awareness of the problems faced by other people around the world. From New York to Karachi, from China to Brazil, it was a message which found its way to the hearts - and to the feet - of millions.

Running all over the world – 50 million people took part in The Race Against Time. (ALLSPORT)

TOP 10 MUSIC VIDEOS

This Week	Last Week	Title	Artist	Label
1	1	IF LOOKS COULD KILL	Heart	(PMI)
2	NEW	THE VIDEO SINGLES	Wet Wet Wet	(Channel 5)
3	2	WHO'S BETTER WHO'S BEST?	Who	(Channel 5)
4	3	THE HARDLINE ACCORDING TO	Terence Trent D'Arby	(CBS/Fox)
5	6	STRANGE	Depeche Mode	(Virgin)
6	5	THE BEST OF OMD	OMD	(Virgin)
7	4	ALWAYS GUARANTEED	Cliff Richard	(PMI)
8	8	VOICE ON VIDEO	Alexander O'Neal	(CBS/Fox)
9	7	MORE VITAL IDOL	Billy Idol	(Chrysalis)
10	13	UNDER A BLOOD RED SKY	U2	(Virgin)

TOP 20 ALBUMS

This Week	Last Week	Title	Artist	Label
1	NEW	NOW THAT'S WHAT I CALL MUSIC 11	Various	(EMI/Virgin/Polygram)
2	1	VIVA HATE	Morrissey	(HMV)
3	2	NAKED	Talking Heads	(EMI)
4	4	THE BEST OF...	OMD	(Virgin)
5	9	FROM LANGLEY PARK TO MEMPHIS	Prefab Sprout	(Kitchenware)
6	NEW	THE STORY OF THE CLASH VOLUME 1	Clash	(CBS)
7	8	HEARSAY	Alexander O'Neal	(Tabu)
8	5	THE HARDLINE ACCORDING TO	Terence Trent D'Arby	(CBS)
9	6	UNFORGETTABLE	Various	(EMI)
10	11	POPPED IN SOULED OUT	Wet Wet Wet	(Precious Organisation)
11	7	GIVE ME THE REASON	Luther Vandross	(Epic)
12	3	TEAR DOWN THESE WALLS	Billy Ocean	(Jive)
13	13	TURN BACK THE CLOCK	Johnny Hates Jazz	(Virgin)
14	10	WHENEVER YOU NEED SOMEBODY	Rick Astley	(RCA)
15	14	HEAVEN ON EARTH	Belinda Carlisle	(Virgin)
16	12	WHO'S BETTER WHO'S BEST?	The Who	(Polydor)
17	22	WHITNEY	Whitney Houston	(Arista)
18	NEW	CHALK MARK ON A RAINSTORM	Joni Mitchell	(Geffen)
19	23	TANGO IN THE NIGHT	Fleetwood Mac	(Warner Brothers)
20	38	HORIZONS	Various	(K-Tel)

TOP 10 SINGLES

WEEK 2

This Week	Last Week	Title	Artist	Label
1	1	DON'T TURN AROUND	Aswad	(Mango)
2	2	DROP THE BOY	Bros	(CBS)
3	15	HEART	Pet Shop Boys	(Parlophone)
4	3	COULD'VE BEEN	Tiffany	(MCA)
5	8	STAY ON THESE ROADS	A-Ha	(Warner Brothers)
6	4	CAN I PLAY WITH MADNESS	Iron Maiden	(EMI)
7	7	CROSS MY BROKEN HEART	Sinitta	(Fanfare)
8	9	I'M NOT SCARED	Eighth Wonder	(CBS)
9	23	LOVE CHANGES EVERYTHING	Climie Fisher	(EMI)
10	13	ONLY IN MY DREAMS	Debbie Gibson	(Atlantic)

WEEK 3

This Week	Last Week	Title	Artist	Label
1	3	HEART	Pet Shop Boys	(Parlophone)
2	2	DROP THE BOY	Bros	(CBS)
3	9	LOVE CHANGES EVERYTHING	Climie Fisher	(EMI)
4	1	DON'T TURN AROUND	Aswad	(Mango)
5	23	EVERYWHERE	Fleetwood Mac	(Warner Brothers)
6	4	COULD'VE BEEN	Tiffany	(MCA)
7	16	DREAMING	Glen Goldsmith	(Reproduction)
8	8	I'M NOT SCARED	Eighth Wonder	(CBS)
9	7	CROSS MY BROKEN HEART	Sinitta	(Fanfare)
10	10	ONLY IN MY DREAMS	Debbie Gibson	(Atlantic)

WEEK 4

This Week	Last Week	Title	Artist	Label
1	1	HEART	Pet Shop Boys	(Parlophone)
2	3	LOVE CHANGES EVERYTHING	Climie Fisher	(EMI)
3	5	EVERYWHERE	Fleetwood Mac	(Warner Brothers)
4	15	WHO'S LEAVING WHO	Hazell Dean	(EMI)
5	2	DROP THE BOY	Bros	(CBS)
6	42	THEME FROM S-EXPRESS	S-Express	(Rhythm King)
7	11	PROVE YOUR LOVE	Taylor Dayne	(Arista)
8	17	PINK CADILLAC	Natalie Cole	(Manhattan)
9	16	GIRLFRIEND	Pebbles	(MCA)
10	20	I WANT YOU BACK	Bananarama	(London)

NETWORK CHART TOP 40

1	1	THEME FROM S-EXPRESS	S-Express	(Rhythm King)
2	9	MARY'S PRAYER	Danny Wilson	(Virgin)
3	21	PERFECT	Fairground Attraction	(RCA)
4	4	PINK CADILLAC	Natalie Cole	(Manhattan)
5	5	I WANT YOU BACK '88	Jackson 5	(Motown)
6	7	I WANT YOU BACK	Bananarama	(London)
7	10	ONE MORE TRY	George Michael	(Epic)
8	6	WHO'S LEAVING WHO	Hazell Dean	(EMI)
9	2	HEART	Pet Shop Boys	(Parlophone)
10	12	THE PAYBACK MIX	James Brown	(Urban)
11	14	A LOVE SUPREME	Will Downing	(4th & Broadway)
12	3	LET'S ALL CHANT	Pat & Mick	(PWL)
13	45	PUMP UP THE BITTER	Starturn on 45 Pints	(Pacific)
14	22	SHE'S LIKE THE WIND	Patrick Swayze & Wendy Fraser	(RCA)
15	15	GET LUCKY	Jermaine Stewart	(Siren)

Fairground Attraction (RETNA)   Fleetwood Mac (WEA)

16	3	LOVE CHANGES	Climie Fisher	(EMI)
17	NEW	BLUE MONDAY 1988	New Order	(Factory)
18	27	OUT OF REACH	Primitives	(Lazy)
19	20	IT TAKES TWO	Robe Base & DJ E-Z Rock	(Citybeat)
20	23	PIANO IN THE DARK	Brenda Russell	(Breakout)
21	NEW	ALPHABET ST.	Prince	(Paisley Park)
22	38	DIVINE EMOTIONS	Narada	(Reprise)
23	8	EVERYWHERE	Fleetwood Mac	(Warner Brothers)
24	11	GIRLFRIEND	Pebbles	(MCA)
25	36	BORN AGAIN	The Christians	(Island)
26	24	I GAVE IT UP	Luther Vandross	(Epic)
27	16	JUST A MIRAGE	Jellybean featuring Adele Bertei	(Chrysalis)
28	40	BROKEN LAND	Adventures	(Elektra)
29	35	WHEN WILL YOU MAKE MY TELEPHONE RING	Deacon Blue	(CBS)
30	18	PROVE YOUR LOVE	Taylor Dayne	(Arista)
31	34	WALK AWAY	Joyce Sims	(London)
32	29	THERE'S ALWAYS SOMETHING THERE TO REMIND ME	Housemartins	(Go! Discs)
33	19	DREAMING	Glen Goldsmith	(Reproduction)
34	33	BEYOND THE PALE	Mission	(Mercury)
35	NEW	LOADSAMONEY	Harry Enfield	(Mercury)
36	48	BEDS ARE BURNING	Midnight Oil	(Sprint)
37	43	NITE AND DAY	Al B Sure	(Warner Brothers)
38	17	DROP THE BOY	Bros	(CBS)
39	59	SOMEWHERE IN MY HEART	Aztec Camera	(WEA)
40	25	COULD'VE BEEN	Tiffany	(MCA)

S-EXPRESS

Way back in 1987, a young London club DJ was bemoaning the lack of what he saw as exciting new records.

"If nobody else starts to make the kind of music that gets people screaming and rushing onto the dance floor again, then I'm just going to have to do it myself."

Yet nobody was more astonished than Mark Moore - for it was he - to find that 12 months later he was as good as his word! Mark was the leading force behind S-Express, whose debut single - "Theme From S-Express" - chugged effortlessly to the top of the Network Chart in May. And despite his super-confidence in his ability to get people dancing, Mark admits he never planned on the impact his record made. After all, it only cost £1,000 to create.

"Originally, we just thought it was going to be a club hit and sell a few thousand copies," he says. "But then we realised it was going to take up a lot more time as it became more successful, so we had to re-think the whole band. The original members couldn't commit themselves. They had jobs and college to go to."

For that reason, the line-up of S-Express appears to have been a confusing and ever-changing one, but lead singer Michelle Ndrika has been there from the start - ever since she was discovered by Mark in a London pizza parlour.

"I'd ordered a pizza and suddenly realised I didn't have enough money to pay for it," she explains. "The only thing I could think of doing was to stand on the table and sing for my supper. Mark walked in at that moment, and loved my voice. He asked me to sing with S-Express - and he even agreed to pay for my pizza!"

At the time, Mark was already a well-known figure on the London club scene, a position he found himself in by pure chance.

"I just fell into all of this," he grins. "I always used to take records to the DJ Tasty Tim at the Wag Club, and then one night he was away. So I did the DJing - and everyone went mad! I became Tim's partner after that."

The musical style of S-Express, a mixture of everything from Seventies disco to hip-hop, is very much a do-it-yourself sound - with various 'bits borrowed' from other records by a technique called sampling. Mark prefers to call the style 'Mutant House' and reckons the attitude behind it owes a lot to the spirit of punk rock.

"It's certainly the best thing that's happened since punk rock," he says, " and there are many similarities between that and what we do. A few years ago, everybody who went to a club wanted to be in a band - nowadays, they all want to be DJs. But the great link is that to do what we do, you don't need to be a musician. Just like punk. It's easy."

And, just like punk, clothes and fashion have played an important part in the ride to success of S-Express, whose customary costume consists of various relics from Seventies' trendiness - including flares, platform boots and psychedelic shirts with big collars.

Mark, however, feels that too much has been made of the way S-Express look, and perhaps not enough of how the group actually sounds.

"There's too much talk about the clothes, and not the music," he says. "It's always the clothes first, music second - but the clothes are just an added attraction."

Mark Moore's ambition is to become a film director, no doubt because he thinks he can make better movies than many now showing. Time will tell...

(RETNA)

S-Express cut clothing bills by everyone wearing the same stuff all at once.

BRITAIN'S BIGGEST EVER TV SHOW

In the wake of pioneering radio fund raising events, ITV embarked on a marathon broadcast in aid of charity when they mounted their Telethon '88.

Beginning at 7pm on Sunday, May 29, the Telethon was transmitted through the night and all the following day before ending at 10pm on Monday evening — by which time a grand total of £21,015,604 had been pledged! The appeal easily topped the £15 million record set by the BBC's Comic Relief three months earlier and also beat the Children In Need Appeal's one day total of £10 million.

The money for the Telethon poured in at £7,500 a minute. Just as staggering as the cash collected were the viewing figures for the 27 hour event of live television. Over 76 per cent of the population tuned in. That's 35 million people — even more than the number who switched on to watch Live Aid.

All of the regional TV companies, from Grampion to Channel and Anglia to Ulster, combined to stage the Telethon and the money raised was allocated to five priority areas nationally ; children, disability, training and employment, special needs — such as homelessness — and self help. Prince Charles, patron of the Independent Broadcasting Telethon Trust, played an important part in getting funds to each cause, but it was the nation which united to raise the much-needed cash. Across the country fund raising schemes and sponsored events helped the cash to come rolling in while celebrities filed on screen one after the other to encourage further contributions from viewers or simply to man the phone lines.

Nobody did more for Telethon '88 than its host, Michael Aspel. He stayed awake and on his feet for the entire duration and when it was all over admitted, "I thought I was going to collapse. Now I will be staging my own sleepathon!"

Meanwhile, Independent Radio stations around the country continued to raise yet more money throughout the year thanks to the enthusiasm of pop stars and D. J.s and the bountiful support of their listeners.

(SYNDICATION INTERNATIONAL)

Michael Aspel – plenty to celebrate after hosting 27 hours of live TV.

FOOTBALL'S FINAL SURPRISES

In all the previous 106 FA Cup Finals, there had never been a victory more unexpected than that achieved by lowly underdogs Wimbledon over Britain's finest soccer side, Liverpool.

The experts all agreed - it was a game which Wimbledon simply could not win - yet a single goal from Lawrie Sanchez in the 37th minute was sufficient to silence all the critics. It also proved that in football - as with any other sport - anything is possible when you try hard enough. Wimbledon won the cup, the most glamourous prize in the English game, just 11 years after climbing out of non-league football.

Sanchez called his team's stunning result a triumph for the ordinary man in the street, while the club's managing director, Sam Hammam, had another message for the world.

"People say our success is a fairy tale," he boomed, "and that makes me unhappy. It was done by hard work."

The same could be said about the equally shocking last-minute victory by Celtic against Dundee United north of the border that afternoon - at the first Scottish FA Cup Final to be attended by a British prime minister in 22 years. And, like its English counterpart - in which Liverpool had a goal disallowed and a penalty saved - it will go down as a classic clash in footballing folklore.

United had a score to settle in the cup. They last fought for the trophy against Celtic in 1985 and were a goal up with 15 minutes to go, only to be beaten 2-1. On the occasion of their centenary year in 1988, Celtic pulled off another escape act - with a winning goal that stole the show just 15 seconds from the final whistle!

As before, the scoreline was Celtic 2 Dundee United 1, and the cup went back to Parkhead, the 28th time the Glasgow team had triumphed in their 45 cup final appearances.

Wimbledon acknowledge the cheers of the Wembley crowd after winning the FA Cup.

(ALLSPORT)

TOP 10 MUSIC VIDEOS

This Week	Last Week	Title	Artist	Label
1	3	THE VIDEO SINGLES	**Wet Wet Wet**	(Channel 5)
2	NEW	VIEW FROM A BRIDGE	**T'Pau**	(Virgin)
3	4	IF LOOKS COULD KILL	**Heart**	(PMI)
4	1	TRILOGY	**Whitesnake**	(PMI)
5	2	STORY TELLING GIANTS	**Talking Heads**	(PMI)
6	NEW	HIP HOP AND RAPPING IN THE HOUSE	**Various**	(Stylus)
7	5	NOW THAT'S WHAT I CALL MUSIC VIDEO II	**Various**	(PMI/Virgin)
8	12	THE HARDLINE ACCORDING TO...	**Terence Trent D'Arby**	(CBS/Fox)
9	18	THE MAKING OF 'THRILLER'	**Michael Jackson**	(Vestron)
10	7	WHO'S BETTER WHO'S BEST?	**The Who**	(Channel 5)

TOP 20 ALBUMS

This Week	Last Week	Title	Artist	Label
1	2	THE INNOCENTS	**Erasure**	(Mute)
2	4	TANGO IN THE NIGHT	**Fleetwood Mac**	(Warner Brothers)
3	5	PUSH	**Bros**	(CBS)
4	3	NOW THAT'S WHAT I CALL MUSIC II	**Various**	(EMI/Virgin/Polygram)
5	11	HIP HOP AND RAPPING IN THE HOUSE	**Various**	(Stylus)
6	6	THE BEST OF...	**OMD**	(Virgin)
7	1	SEVENTH SON OF A SEVENTH SON	**Iron Maiden**	(EMI)
8	7	DIRTY DANCING	**Soundtrack**	(RCA)
9	75	NITELIFE	**Various**	(CBS)
10	9	ACTUALLY	**Pet Shop Boys**	(Parlophone)
11	8	POPPED IN SOULED OUT	**Wet Wet Wet**	(Precious Organisation)
12	14	EVERYTHING	**Climie Fisher**	(EMI)
13	12	THE HARDLINE ACCORDING TO...	**Terence Trent D'Arby**	(CBS)
14	10	BARBED WIRE KISSES	**Jesus & Mary Chain**	(blanco y negro)
15	20	WILL DOWNING	**Will Downing**	(4th & Broadway)
16	15	BRIDGE OF SPIES	**T'Pau**	(Siren)
17	19	THE CHRISTIANS	**The Christians**	(Chrysalis)
18	17	WHITNEY	**Whitney Houston**	(Arista)
19	27	FAITH	**George Michael**	(Epic)
20	16	HEAVEN ON EARTH	**Belinda Carlisle**	(Virgin)

TOP 10 SINGLES

WEEK 2

This Week	Last Week	Title	Artist	Label
1	3	PERFECT	**Fairground Attraction**	(RCA)
2	1	THEME FROM S-EXPRESS	**S-Express**	(Rhythm King)
3	17	BLUE MONDAY '88	**New Order**	(Factory)
4	2	MARY'S PRAYER	**Danny Wilson**	(Virgin)
5	21	ALPHABET ST.	**Prince**	(Paisley Park)
6	35	LOADSAMONEY	**Harry Enfield**	(Mercury)
7	13	PUMP UP THE BITTER	**Starturn On 45 Pints**	(Pacific)
8	8	WHO'S LEAVING WHO	**Hazell Dean**	(EMI)
9	4	PINK CADILLAC	**Natalie Cole**	(Manhattan)
10	6	I WANT YOU BACK	**Bananarama**	(London)

WEEK 3

This Week	Last Week	Title	Artist	Label
1	3	PERFECT	**Fairground Attraction**	(RCA)
2	40	WITH A LITTLE HELP FROM MY FRIENDS / SHE'S LEAVING HOME	**Wet Wet Wet/ Billy Bragg**	(Childline)
3	3	BLUE MONDAY '88	**New Order**	(Factory)
4	6	LOADSAMONEY	**Harry Enfield**	(Mercury)
5	2	THEME FROM S-EXPRESS	**S-Express**	(Rhythm King)
6	5	ALPHABET ST.	**Prince**	(Paisley Park)
7	69	ANFIELD RAP	**Liverpool FC**	(Virgin)
8	7	PUMP UP THE BITTER	**Starturn On 45 Pints**	(Pacific)
9	50	GOT TO BE CERTAIN	**Kylie Minogue**	(PWL)
10	4	MARY'S PRAYER	**Danny Wilson**	(Virgin)

WEEK 4

This Week	Last Week	Title	Artist	Label
1	2	WITH A LITTLE HELP FROM MY FRIENDS / SHE'S LEAVING HOME	**Wet Wet Wet/ Billy Bragg**	(Childline)
2	1	PERFECT	**Fairground Attraction**	(RCA)
3	9	GOT TO BE CERTAIN	**Kylie Minogue**	(PWL)
4	7	ANFIELD RAP	**Liverpool FC**	(Virgin)
5	3	BLUE MONDAY '88	**New Order**	(Factory)
6	4	LOADSAMONEY	**Harry Enfield**	(Mercury)
7	11	DIVINE EMOTIONS	**Narada**	(Reprise)
8	5	THEME FROM S-EXPRESS	**S-Express**	(Rhythm King)
9	30	DON'T GO	**Hothouse Flowers**	(London)
10	19	CIRCLE IN THE SAND	**Belinda Carlisle**	(Virgin)

NEW ORDER

There has never been a record quite like "Blue Monday" by New Order.

Originally released in 1983, it has exceeded sales of 2 million worldwide - more than 800,000 of them in Britain alone - and spent four uninterrupted years in the Top 200, while going on to become the biggest-selling 12-inch single in the history of recording.

In May, the song's by now familiar sound was again heard in the Top Ten following its third release - this time as a 7-inch. All of this appears to mean little or nothing to the publicity-shy members of the Manchester group that previously answered to the name of Joy Division until the death of lead singer Ian Curtis in May, 1980.

The remaining members, Peter Hook, Steven Morris and Bernard Albrecht, then changed their collective title to New Order and hired Gillian Gilbert to play keyboards, but the doomy, depressing aura which surrounded Joy Division remains with them to this day. It's an image perpetuated by a reputation for being 'difficult'. Doing interviews is definitely low on the New Order list of priorities.

"If you're a loud person in Manchester, you tend to get beaten up," Bernard offers by way of some form of explanation.

Silent or not, New Order are major celebrities in their home city, where the group's huge success has bought it co-ownership of Manchester's trend-setting night club, The Hacienda.

New Order prefer to mind their own business and expect other people to do the same - and if they don't, they may have Peter Hook to contend with.

"I always wear leather," he says. "You don't mess with someone in leather if they've got the right walk. I walk like I mean business - and I do!"

(RETNA)

New Order – four cheeseburgers
and a strawberry milkshake, please!

(RETNA)

NETWORK CHART TOP 40

(RETNA)

THE
NETWORK
CHART
SHOW

Belinda Carlisle

(RETNA)

Hothouse Flowers

1	1	WITH A LITTLE HELP FROM MY FRIENDS......	**Wet Wet Wet**	
		SHE'S LEAVING HOME	**Billy Bragg**	(Childline)
2	3	GOT TO BE CERTAIN...............................	**Kylie Minogue**...	(PWL)
3	14	CHECK THIS OUT	**L.A. Mix**...	(Breakout)
4	10	CIRCLE IN THE SAND.................................	**Belinda Carlisle**	(Virgin)
5	2	PERFECT...	**Fairground Attraction**	(RCA)
6	9	DON'T GO	**Hothouse Flowers**	(London)
7	11	THE KING OF ROCK 'N' ROLL.......................	**Prefab Sprout**	(Kitchenware)
8	12	SOMEWHERE IN MY HEART........................	**Aztec Camera**..	(WEA)
9	19	MY ONE TEMPTATION..................................	**Mica Paris**.......................................	(4th & Broadway)
10	5	BLUE MONDAY '88	**New Order**..	(Factory)
11	18	IM NIN'ALU	**Ofra Haza**...	(WEA)
12	23	OH PATTI DON'T FEEL SORRY FOR LOVERBOY	**Scritti Politti**	(Virgin)
13	7	DIVINE EMOTIONS	**Narada**..	(Reprise)
14	16	WHAT ABOUT LOVE.....................................	**Heart**...	(Capitol)
15	30	LOVE WILL SAVE THE DAY..........................	**Whitney Houston**	(Arista)
16	8	THEME FROM S-EXPRESS...........................	**S-Express**..	(Rhythm King)
17	25	OUT OF THE BLUE..	**Debbie Gibson**..	(Atlantic)
18	20	THIS IS ME	**Climie Fisher**..	(EMI)
19	13	BAD YOUNG BROTHER..................................	**Derek B**...	(Tuff Audio)
20	6	LOADSAMONEY	**Harry Enfield**	(Mercury)
21	27	GIVE A LITTLE LOVE	**Aswad**	(Mango)
22	4	ANFIELD RAP	**Liverpool FC**..	(Virgin)
23	26	VOYAGE VOYAGE...	**Desireless**...	(CBS)
24	39	LIFE AT A TOP PEOPLE'S HEALTH FARM	**Style Council**..	(Polydor)
25	55	LOST IN YOU	**Rod Stewart**	(Warner Brothers)
26	NEW	THE LOVERS...	**Alexander O'Neal**	(Tabu)
27	15	BROKEN LAND...	**Adventures**	(Elektra)
28	73	MOVIN' 1988	**Brass Construction**	(Syncopate)
29	63	GET IT	**Stevie Wonder & Michael Jackson**	(Motown)
30	NEW	ANOTHER WEEKEND	**5 Star**..	(Tent)
31	21	I WANT YOU BACK	**Bananarama**..	(London)
32	NEW	MERCEDES BOY	**Pebbles**...	(MCA)
33	NEW	DOCTORIN' THE TARDIS..............................	**Timelords**	(KLF)
34	60	THE VALLEY ROAD	**Bruce Hornsby & The Range**	(RCA)
35	32	HEY MR HEARTACHE....................................	**Kim Wilde**..	(MCA)
36	50	DON'T CALL ME BABY	**Voice Of The Beehive**	(London)
37	37	NAUGHTY GIRLS	**Samantha Fox**	(Jive)
38	33	RUN'S HOUSE...	**Run D.M.C.**	(London)
39	57	LITTLE FIFTEEN	**Depeche Mode**	(Mute)
40	40	WHO GETS THE LOVE?.................................	**Status Quo**	(Vertigo)

WET WET WET

NUMBER ① ONE ACT

The simple formula often used to revive a flagging career or generate an instant hit is just to take a well-known song and record a new version. But there are two major reasons why this didn't apply to Wet Wet Wet's version of the 20-year-old Beatles' song, "With A Little Help From My Friends".

Firstly, the Glaswegian band was already in a position of secured popularity and had no need to make a 'comeback'. Secondly, and far more importantly, the pin-up favourites only agreed to sing the song at all in the name of charity. In this case, it was to raise money for Childline, Britain's first ever telephone helpline for children in danger.

The group - singer Marti Pellow, drummer Tommy Cunningham, bass guitarist Graeme Clark and keyboard player Neil Mitchell - became involved with the cause when they were asked to take part in a compilation album called "Sgt. Pepper Knew My Father" - an updated version of the classic "Sgt. Pepper's Lonely Hearts Club Band" LP by The Beatles.

"We'd been approached to do work for loads of charities before," Tommy remembers, "but this one was particularly important to us.

"Childline is aimed at children who are victims of sexual and physical abuse. They get 8,000 calls a year, but only 2,000 can get through because of a lack of phone lines. Our single selling copies will help them to run more lines. We saw a chance to do something positive with the record, we wanted to do something to help - and music is what we do best. It's a great song, too! It really says it all."

The Wets also had another motive for lending their name to Childline and it lay far closer to home.

"Charity is very important to Wet Wet Wet," Tommy explains, "because that's how we started, really. We had no equipment at all, but other people lent it to us. Glasgow is like that. People scratch your back, and you scratch theirs. To me, that is a form of charity - and the fact that we are from Glasgow is what inspired us all to try music."

Far from it being an effortless glide to the top, the Wet Wet Wet story is one of false starts, frustration and disappointment. It began at Clydebank High School, where Graeme formed the group when all of its members were 15 or 16. Coming from an area in which jobs were few and far between, they all saw music as an escape. Only Tommy made a serious attempt to secure a 'proper' job as a joiner.

"Our only real options were to play football, snooker or music," he reckons. "That was it. What motivated us to pick up instruments in the first place was to do something other than just sit about or walk the streets."

So, for three years, the group collected dole money and faithfully rehearsed their music in Graeme's living room. By early · 1985, their first demo tape had nine major record companies fran-

tically bidding for their signatures on a recording contract.

"It was bizarre," Graeme recalls. "The first man who tried to sign us bought us a pint of lager and we thought it was brilliant. We would have signed our lives to him!"

Instead, the group took its time and eventually chose Phonogram - but it was two years before the debut single from Wet Wet Wet was released. And by the time "Wishing I Was Lucky" finally did become available, the lads were already in debt to the tune of £500,000.

The intervening years and a lot of sheer hard work has put the group back on course - with a string of hit singles and a debut album, "Popped In Souled Out", which has sold 1.2 million copies in Britain alone. But Wet Wet Wet say they have learned never to take anything for granted.

"We're just four working class boys from Glasgow who got hold of a chance," says Marti. "We all grabbed it with both hands as tightly as we could, got our heads down and ran - and that's what we're still doing..."

(RETNA)

Wet Wet Wet might have played football or snooker instead!

(SYNDICATION INTERNATIONAL)

POLITICS GOES POP AT WEMBLEY

The frequently voiced theory that pop music should have nothing whatsoever to do with politics and should never be mixed with politics was ground into the dust on June 11 - if only for ten hours.

That was how long the Nelson Mandela 70th Birthday Tribute concert at Wembley Stadium lasted, and for the duration, 74,000 people in the audience and an estimated one billion watching the action on TV had more on their minds than who would sing what song next. True, there were many who had no knowledge of Nelson Mandela before the event - some even thought he was a performer at the concert - but by the end of the day, few were left in doubt about his identity, his achievements or what he represented. And that was the point of it all.

Unlike Live Aid, the Mandela extravaganza was not about raising money for charity - though some was collected in his name - it was concerned with raising public awareness of one man's fight for freedom. Nelson Mandela was jailed 26 years ago for conspiring to overthrow the apartheid system in South Africa.

His plight, and his 70th birthday, provided the inspiration for the concert - at which all the performing musicians, including Dire Straits, George Michael, Simple Minds, Stevie Wonder, Whitney Houston and Phil Collins gave their services free of charge.

The day also witnessed the birth of an international star in American singer-songwriter Tracy Chapman. She played two short sets clutching an acoustic guitar and found herself booming in popularity quite literally overnight. It was appropriate, the concert's director Ken O'Neill felt, that she of all people should have been so favourably singled out.

"I think part of her appeal was her bravery as a new artist standing out there almost alone in front of millions - the vast majority of whom didn't know who she was," he said. "Tracy Chapman just captured the spirit of the day, somehow."

(SYNDICATION INTERNATIONAL)

WIMBLEDON'S GIANT KILLERS

Martina Navratilova called it "the end of a chapter" and it was the right hand of Steffi Graf which turned the final page.

Bidding for an historic ninth consecutive Wimbledon title, the once invincible American was finally broken on the Centre Court - and with defeat came an end to a record 47 straight wins in the championship. The player who beat her 5-7, 6-2, 6-1 was just 11 years old when Martina clinched her first Wimbledon crown!

Steffi Graf has come a long way since she took up the game at the age of four, using a sawn-off junior racket to hit balls at her father over a settee which took the place of a net - and her triumph in the world's greatest tennis tournament was just part of a winning streak in 1988 that may never be equalled.

The West German multi-millionairess became only the fourth woman ever to complete the Grand Slam - capturing the Australian, French and American Opens along with Wimbledon in one season - and then went one better. In September she won the first Olympic gold medal on offer to women's tennis in 64 years.

Only Stefan Edberg from Sweden came between a double celebration for the Germans at Wimbledon, when he prevented Boris Becker from taking a third title in a disappointingly one-sided match that ended 4-6, 7-6, 6-4, 6-2.

Edberg became the first Swede to win the championship since the great Bjorn Borg - and the London-based 22-year-old did it with the help of British coach and former Davis Cup captain Tony Pickard.

The son of a police chief, Edberg marked his win in style; flat on his back and kicking his legs in the air on court after the final point. He then determined to keep his feet squarely on the ground once the excitement had died down.

"I had a nice quiet life before," he said, "and I want to keep having one. I won't change."

Becker's words served up an equally defiant promise.

"That trophy is only out on loan as far as I'm concerned!"

Stefi Graf's fantastic year included a historic Grand Slam and an Olympic gold medal.
(SYNDICATION INTERNATIONAL)

TOP 10 MUSIC VIDEOS

THIS WEEK	LAST WEEK			
1	2	THE VIDEO SINGLES	Wet Wet Wet	(Channel 5)
2	1	VIEW FROM A BRIDGE	T'Pau	(Virgin)
3	6	IF LOOKS COULD KILL	Heart	(PMI)
4	NEW	CLIFF' EM ALL	Metallica	(Polygram)
5	3	STORY TELLING GIANTS	Talking Heads	(PMI)
6	4	TRILOGY	Whitesnake	(PMI)
7	NEW	RUNNING THE DISTANCE	Curiosity Killed The Cat	(Channel 5)
8	5	GLASS SPIDER TOUR	David Bowie	(Video Col.)
9	NEW	VIDEOS IN THE RAW	W.A.S.P.	(PMI)
10	10	LIVE	Terence Trent D'Arby	(CBS/Fox)

TOP 20 ALBUMS

1	2	TANGO IN THE NIGHT	Fleetwood Mac	(Warner Brothers)
2	19	NITELIFE	Various	(CBS)
3	4	MORE DIRTY DANCING	Various	(RCA)
4	9	WHITNEY	Whitney Houston	(Arista)
5	1	LOVESEXY	Prince	(Paisley Park)
6	NEW	OU812	Van Halen	(Warner Brothers)
7	6	THE FIRST OF A MILLION KISSES	Fairground Attraction	(RCA)
8	25	HEAVEN ON EARTH	Belinda Carlisle	(Virgin)
9	NEW	OUT OF ORDER	Rod Stewart	(Warner Brothers)
10	8	DIRTY DANCING	Soundtrack	(RCA)
11	5	STRONGER THAN PRIDE	Sade	(Epic)
12	12	POPPED IN SOULED OUT	Wet Wet Wet	(Precious Organisation)
13	3	THE CHRISTIANS	The Christians	(Island)
14	7	MOTOWN DANCE PARTY	Various	(Motown)
15	17	SCENES FROM THE SOUTHSIDE	Bruce Hornsby & The Range	(RCA)
16	NEW	TOUGHER THAN LEATHER	Run DMC	(Profile)
17	16	FROM LANGLEY PARK TO MEMPHIS	Prefab Sprout	(Kitchenware)
18	10	SIXTIES MIX TWO	Various	(Stylus)
19	15	BULLET FROM A GUN	Derek B	(Tuff Audio)
20	11	NOW THAT'S WHAT I CALL QUITE GOOD	Housemartins	(Go! Discs)

TOP 10 SINGLES

WEEK 2

1	1	WITH A LITTLE HELP FROM MY FRIENDS / SHE'S LEAVING HOME	Wet Wet Wet / Billy Bragg	(Childline)
2	2	GOT TO BE CERTAIN	Kylie Minogue	(PWL)
3	3	CHECK THIS OUT	L.A. Mix	(Breakout)
4	33	DOCTORIN' THE TARDIS	Timelords	(KLF)
5	8	SOMEWHERE IN MY HEART	Aztec Camera	(WEA)
6	4	CIRCLE IN THE SAND	Belinda Carlisle	(Virgin)
7	23	VOYAGE VOYAGE	Desireless	(CBS)
8	9	MY ONE TEMPTATION	Mica Paris	(4th & Broadway)
9	15	LOVE WILL SAVE THE DAY	Whitney Houston	(Arista)
10	7	THE KING OF ROCK 'N' ROLL	Prefab Sprout	(Kitchenware)

WEEK 3

1	4	DOCTORIN' THE TARDIS	The Timelords	(KLF)
2	1	WITH A LITTLE HELP FROM MY FRIENDS / SHE'S LEAVING HOME	Wet Wet Wet / Billy Bragg	(Childline)
3	7	VOYAGE VOYAGE	Desireless	(CBS)
4	2	GOT TO BE CERTAIN	Kylie Minogue	(PWL)
5	NEW	I OWE YOU NOTHING	Bros	(CBS)
6	34	BOYS	Sabrina	(Ibiza)
7	15	I SAW HIM STANDING THERE	Tiffany	(MCA)
8	5	SOMEWHERE IN MY HEART	Aztec Camera	(WEA)
9	18	EVERY DAY IS LIKE SUNDAY	Morrissey	(HMV)
10	8	MY ONE TEMPTATION	Mica Paris	(4th & Broadway)

WEEK 4

1	5	I OWE YOU NOTHING	Bros	(CBS)
2	1	DOCTORIN' THE TARDIS	The Timelords	(KLF)
3	6	BOYS	Sabrina	(Ibiza)
4	3	VOYAGE VOYAGE	Desireless	(CBS)
5	1	1WILD WORLD	Maxi Priest	(10)
6	2	WITH A LITTLE HELP FROM MY FRIENDS / SHE'S LEAVING HOME	Wet Wet Wet / Billy Bragg	(Childline)
7	59	THE TWIST (YO TWIST)	The Fat Boys & Chubby Checker	(Urban)
8	12	CHAINS OF LOVE	Erasure	(Mute)
9	23	TRIBUTE (RIGHT ON)	Pasadenas	(CBS)
10	9	EVERY DAY IS LIKE SUNDAY	Morrissey	(HMV)

TOP TEN ACT
PREFAB SPROUT

There have been many ridiculous refrains in the course of pop history, but none, perhaps, so daft as... "Hot dog, jumping frog, Albuquerque..."

That immortal nonsense provided the chorus to "The King of Rock and Roll", the Network Chart Top Ten debut for a Newcastle group with an equally silly name - Prefab Sprout. Yet, despite all the joking, the music made by singer Paddy McAloon, his brother Martin, Neil Conti and Wendy Smith has for years been widely acclaimed as almost too adult and too intelligent to be successful.

So it comes as a surprise to learn that Paddy, who once referred to himself as "probably the greatest songwriter in the world", actually took just 20 minutes to create "The King of Rock and Roll".

"I got off the bus one day, picked up the guitar and wrote it," he says simply. "I thought it was so funny that I couldn't play it to anyone. It was so ridiculous that, at first, we couldn't record it."

Paddy first dreamed up the name Prefab Sprout in 1973, while he was still a long way from finishing school. He says it was inspired by the wonder he felt at seeing others like Tyrannosaurus Rex,.

"When you haven't been used to those sort of names, there is a real mystery to them," he explains. "So I put two words together that didn't mean anything, because I figured people would say 'What does it mean?' Mind you, I had other names at the time - like Chrysalis Cognosci!"

Prefab Sprout's career began when the group signed to the Newcastle record company Kitchenware - a hotbed of local talent which also includes Martin Stephenson and The Daintees and Hurrah! Having secured a local recording contract, there was no way Paddy could be lured south by the bright lights of London.

"It's a problem being dislocated from the music business where we live," he admits, "but if I can write songs at home, there's no reason for me to be in London. I don't want to hang around there pretending to be a pop star!"

Prefab Sprout sounds silly enough but they were nearly called Chrysalis Cognosci!
(RETNA)

THE NESCAFÉ NETWORK

THE NETWORK CHART SHOW

Eddie Kidd makes a hit at the Nescafé Fashion Show in London.

If you're one of the thousands of people who have got down for some serious good times with David Jensen and the Nescafé Network Chart Show Roadshow, you'll know all about the fun, freebies, famous faces and of course, the chart-topping sounds spun by David Jensen himself.

But if you've missed out on the greatest Roadshow on earth – listen up and find out what to expect when it takes your area by storm.

In 1985, Nescafé, makers of the nation's favourite coffee and sponsors of the nation's favourite Chart Show, decided to take the show on the road – and do it in style!

In the last four years, David Jensen and the crew have raced around the country, taking the Roadshow into 60 nightclubs across the UK – with a little help from the 43 independent local radio stations that broadcast the show.

"I don't usually like travelling," says David, the man who has presented the Roadshow as far North as Edinburgh in conjunction with Radio Forth, as far South as Plymouth, and even crossed the Irish Sea to visit Downtown Radio in Belfast. "But travelling with the Roadshow is different. I know that at the end of the journey there will be fantastic attendances, with queues of people outside the clubs, and that the Roadshow will be great fun. We all really enjoy doing them, they're a real laugh."

Before the Roadshow takes place, however, there's lots to be done. While the crew go to the club to set up the special lights and effects, David rushes off to the local newspapers and radio station to talk about the evening's Roadshow. After grabbing a bite to eat with the bands who'll be guesting at the gig, there's just time for a quick shower back at the hotel before whizzing off to the Roadshow venue. That's when the fun really starts.

"Nescafé put a lot into the Roadshows to make sure they're all a huge success," says Jensen. As well as being able to strut their stuff to the latest chart sounds, nobody goes home empty handed.

"When I'm on stage I give away hundreds of Nescafé Network Chart Show Roadshow t-shirts, mugs, boxer shorts, watches – loads of freebies," David laughs. "Everybody gets something." In fact, over £500 of merchandise is given away at each gig.

So there's fun and freebies, but what about those famous faces – besides the one sported by Mr Jensen? Roadshow guests have ranged from artists already enjoying chart success, such as Sinitta and Hazell Dean, to acts who are 'bubbling under', like habit (sic) and Blue Mercedes. Those who attended the launch of the 1988 Roadshow UK Tour, at Japanese Whispers, Barnsley, got a real transatlantic treat. American chart duo, Rob Base and D.J. E-Z Rock flew in from the States especially to appear, and took the place by storm with their unique rap-scratch sound.

Jensen is justifiably proud of the Roadshow's track record of forecasting which acts will be successful, and providing them with a showcase for their talents.

"Groups like Breathe, Brother Beyond, Johnny Hates Jazz and Curiosity Killed The Cat have all performed at Roadshows and then made it big," he says.

Another artist that felt the benefits from a Roadshow appearance is Mandy Smith. Mandy raised a few temperatures when she performed her latest release at Rinaldo's Nightclub in Peterborough, wearing a skimpy stage costume.

"Doing the Roadshow helped me get the coverage needed to get my song played on the radio," says Mandy. "So often, the radio playlists can be restrictive – they mainly feature the Top 40."

After performing her set, Mandy stayed on for the highlight of the Rinaldo's/Hereward Radio promotion – a fashion extravaganza featuring the

WEE RULE..! David Jensen introducing Roadshow favourites Total S and TY Tim, The Wee Papa Girl Rappers.

CHART SHOW ON THE ROAD

As well as enjoying the Roadshow in Blackpool with Red Rose Radio, Brother Beyond took time out to chance their luck on the Golden Mile.

David Jensen enjoys a chat with Mandy Smith.

One of 1988's success stories – Breathe – appeared on the Roadshow with Radio Hallam.

Radio City hosted the Roadshow and Blue Mercedes drove the Warrington fans wild.

creations of budding local designers. "I had a great time," says Mandy, who presented the winning designer with a cheque for £100.

The Fashion Show was just one of the more unusual attractions lined up by the Roadshow promotion team. Other out-of-the-ordinary gigs have included a roller disco, and a Roadshow on Ice!

"I really enjoyed it when we went to the Deeside Leisure Centre in Wrexham," Jensen recalls. "I used to play ice-hockey in Canada so I was out there skating too!"

Apart from the prospect of their star D.J. coming a cropper in the rink, the Roadshow team have had few real causes for concern during their tours. Things have run smoothly on-stage at every venue. But there has been one near disaster behind the scenes. The Wee Papa Girl Rappers, a favourite with Roadshow audiences, tell of how they nearly missed their chance to perform at all.

"When we went to Bolton to do the Ritzy/Piccadilly Radio Roadshow we were both really tired," remember TY Tim and Total S. "We had dinner with David Jensen and then had an hour to go back to our hotel before we were due at the club. We thought if we took showers, it would wake us up and make us feel better. The next thing we knew, the phone was ringing with someone on the end saying 'Where are you? You're supposed to be on!' We just threw on our clothes and ran out. We got to the club still damp from the shower!"

The Wee Papa's missed Jensen's slot, but made it in time for Piccadilly's Becky Want to introduce them – to the delight of an enthusiastic audience.

"We want to do loads more Roadshows," say the girls. "It's great of Nescafé to do them for the kids, they really enjoy them and so do we. The Roadshows are fun!"

And the fun, like the show, will go on. With the help of the independent radio stations, D.J.s, clubs, promoters and the stars of The Network Chart Show itself, The Nescafé Network Chart Show Roadshow is gearing up to rock the UK for another successful year. It's new, it's now, it's not to be missed – and it's coming to a club near you!

There is always loads of Fun and lots of Freebies on the Nescafé Network Chart Show Roadshow.

NETWORK CHART TOP 40

1	1	*I OWE YOU NOTHING*	**Bros**	(CBS)
2	7	*THE TWIST (YO TWIST)*	**Fat Boys & Chubby Checker**	(Urban)
3	3	*BOYS*	**Sabrina**	(Ibiza)
4	9	*TRIBUTE (RIGHT ON)*	**Pasadenas**	(CBS)
5	14	*IN THE AIR TONIGHT '88*	**Phil Collins**	(Virgin)
6	2	*DOCTORIN' THE TARDIS*	**The Timelords**	(KLF)
7	21	*BREAKFAST IN BED*	**UB40 with Chrissie Hynde**	(DEP International)
8	5	*WILD WORLD*	**Maxi Priest**	(10)
9	4	*VOYAGE VOYAGE*	**Desireless**	(CBS)
10	40	*PUSH IT/TRAMP*	**Salt 'n' Pepa**	(London/Champion)
11	24	*TOUGHER THAN THE REST*	**Bruce Springsteen**	(CBS)
12	8	*CHAINS OF LOVE*	**Erasure**	(Mute)
13	49	*NOTHING'S GONNA CHANGE MY LOVE FOR YOU*	**Glenn Medeiros**	(London)
14	33	*FAST CAR*	**Tracy Chapman**	(Elektra)
15	16	*CAR WASH*	**Rose Royce**	(MCA)
16	6	*WITH A LITTLE HELP FROM MY FRIENDS* / *SHE'S LEAVING HOME*	**Wet Wet Wet/ Billy Bragg**	(Childline)
17	17	*YOU HAVE PLACED A CHILL IN MY HEART*	**Eurythmics**	(RCA)
18	15	*DON'T BLAME IT ON THAT GIRL*	**Matt Bianco**	(WEA)
19	10	*EVERY DAY IS LIKE SUNDAY*	**Morrissey**	(HMV)
20	43	*MAYBE*	**Hazell Dean**	(EMI)
21	11	*GOT TO BE CERTAIN*	**Kylie Minogue**	(PWL)
22	26	*THERE'S MORE TO LOVE*	**Communards**	(London)
23	54	*I WILL BE WITH YOU*	**T'Pau**	(Siren)
24	12	*SOMEWHERE IN MY HEART*	**Aztec Camera**	(WEA)
25	19	*DON'T CALL ME BABY*	**Voice Of The Beehive**	(London)
26	60	*NEVER TEAR US APART*	**INXS**	(Mercury)
27	20	*THE BLOOD THAT MOVES THE BODY*	**A-Ha**	(Warner Brothers)
28	34	*ATMOSPHERE 1979*	**Joy Division**	(Factory)
29	NEW	*DON'T BELIEVE THE HYPE*	**Public Enemy**	(Def Jam)
30	73	*EVERLASTING*	**Natalie Cole**	(EMI Manhattan)
31	13	*I SAW HIM STANDING THERE*	**Tiffany**	(MCA)
32	32	*WHAT YOU SEE IS WHAT YOU GET*	**Glen Goldsmith**	(Reproduction)
33	27	*PARADISE*	**Sade**	(Epic)
34	18	*LUCRETIA MY REFLECTION*	**Sisters Of Mercy**	(Merciful Release)
35	59	*ROSES ARE RED*	**Mac Band featuring the Mc Campbell Brothers**	(MCA)
36	37	*I DON'T WANNA GO ON WITH YOU LIKE THAT*	**Elton John**	(Rocket)
38	23	*CIRCLE IN THE SAND*	**Belinda Carlisle**	(Virgin)
39	25	*GIVE A LITTLE LOVE*	**Aswad**	(Mango)
40	22	*MY ONE TEMPTATION*	**Mica Paris**	(4th & Broadway)

(LONDON)

Salt 'n' Pepa

BROS

If it's possible to lay claim to a whole year and call it your own, then 1988 most definitely belongs to Bros.

From the beginning of January when Matt, Luke and Craig leapt into the chart with their debut hit single "When Will I Be Famous?" the lads could do no wrong. Rounding off the year in December with four sell-out concerts at Wembley arena and yet another chart hit, "Cat Among The Pigeons/Silent Night" **(peaking** at No 2), the three friends from Collingwood School had experienced the most amazing twelve months of their entire lives.

One of the highlights of 1988 for them was their first Network Chart No 1 in July - "I Owe You Nothing". The first Bros No 1 was almost as big a thrill for the fans as it was for Matt, Luke and Craig. The faithful followed in hordes wherever their idols went but even more overwhelming than the constant attention of the Brosettes was the scale of the achievements towards which those fans pushed Bros. Five consecutive Top Five singles, a chart-topping first album, Push, and the debut UK tour which sold out in less than an hour!

Having conquered Britain, Bros took on the rest of the world, playing to packed houses in Australia, Japan and Europe before returning to the UK for some more sell-out home dates. The effect of so much hard work and the pressure of being constantly in the public eye would be taxing enough for the most experienced of entertainers, but Bros took it all in their stride, despite their lack of years.

The Goss twins, after all, weren't twenty years old until September (1988) and Craig Logan only kissed his teenage years goodbye in March (1989). For all that, the members of Bros seem to have coped remarkably well with this crazy year!

"People are now asking us, 'When will the bubble burst?'" says Luke, "but nobody knows the answer. All we know for sure is that we're enjoying it while it's here. All of this has happened so fast - it's only been months but it seems like years. We've been working so hard, but we're not complaining. I'm a lucky guy - we all are - but you've got to want this as much as we wanted it for there to be a chance of it ever happening."

Bros say they have been chasing stardom ever since they were 12-year-olds. It was then that Matt asked a complete stranger to lend him 50p for a school lunch, and rewarded his new friend Craig Logan by asking him to join the group he had formed with Luke.

They practised together all through school - and by the fifth form they already had a manager - but it wasn't until they left that music became a full-time diversion and the trio began playing in working men's clubs. It was after one such performance that Nicky Graham - now the Bros producer - got to hear about them and recommended that an old friend should see them.

He was Tom Watkins, also manager of The Pet Shop Boys, and after meeting the three hopeful lads, he agreed to look after their career, too. Within a matter of months, Matt, Luke and Craig had been given the name Bros and signed a deal with CBS Records. The rest, as the saying goes, is history, but Craig is still pinching himself to check that he is actually part of it.

"We all are," he admits. "We're bound to. It's one thing saying 'Our ambition is to be the biggest pop group in the world', but it's another kettle of fish altogether when you can actually look around you and see that it's not such an outrageous idea after all!"

Even now that he knows his boyhood dreams are coming true, Matt still can't believe what has happened to him - but he's certain that the most enjoyable aspect of being in Bros is the response from the devoted followers who made it all possible in the first place.

"There's so much love involved in Bros and the people who support us," he says, "and we've got so many of them behind us. As long as they are there, I'll be able to cope with everything else..."

After such a sensational year for Bros, Craig's health problems troubled the group in '89.

(CBS)

THOUSANDS DIE IN SEAL PLAGUE

The first, pitiful signs of the cruel epidemic were noticed by inhabitants of the tiny Danish island of Anholt, midway between Denmark and Sweden.

Standing there on the sandy beach, they had been eagerly awaiting the arrival of the harbour seals which breed locally each year - and instead reeled in horror as hundreds of the dead and dying mammals began washing ashore. Lighthouse keeper Einar Bosen and other islanders were soon picking up dozens of corpses a day. "We've started calling ourselves the death patrol," he said sadly.

In a matter of weeks it became obvious that the plague was spreading. By July, the loss of seals had reached a level which threatened to wipe them from the face of the earth - and the trail of death was on its way to Britain.

Here the common seal population - believed to number at least 25,000 - amounted to about half of the European total, and the future of them all was in doubt. The scale of the catastrophe can be gauged by the death toll in Sweden, where 73 per cent of their common seals died in the Baltic Sea, and in Denmark where around 80 per cent in the North and Baltic Seas were lost.

The cause of the disease was identified as a form of canine distemper virus. The disease can be fatal in dogs,but is kept in check in Britain through vaccination. For various reasons, it would be impossible to vaccinate every wild seal, but the RSPCA and Greenpeace have worked closely together to find a solution to the problem.

The two organisations set up a "seal hospital" in Norfolk in response to the crisis. They have carried out a great deal of research and have had some success in nursing sick seals back to health. This endows the animals with a natural immunity to the disease and allows them to be returned to the wild. The 'hospitals' unfortunately can only handle 30 'cases' at a time.

Captive seals, of course, can be vaccinated, but the virus will continue to take its toll amongst the wild population, threatening one of the world's best loved creatures with extinction. The virus is transmitted by contact, and it can kill within 48 hours.

(SYNDICATION INTERNATIONAL)

(ALLSPORT)

FASHION ON THE MOVE

As they pedalled for glory up mountain roads and through cobbled streets, it probably never occurred to the cyclists in the 75th Tour de France to check out how trendy they looked!

Cuts and grazes from crashes and collisions, sweat from the efforts of their exertions and - in some cases - tears cried through the sheer pain of it all would have been what most of the riders would have seen had they looked in a mirror.

But the physical or emotional discomfort of the riders was the last aspect of their condition which the fashion world noticed as the tour raced its way through 2,003 miles of French scenery. What the designers of the world were busily spotting was... the clothes. Colourful, tight-fitting and light to wear, cycling gear proved to be the fashion craze of summer '88. Outfits from the street - or, at least, from the road - which could safely be worn without any of the agony suffered by its original models, were the things to be seen in.

So, cycling shorts and tops and caps and sweatbands became trendy, while those who donned them were perfectly happy to leave the gruelling business of actually putting the garments through their paces to the tour's overall winner, Pedro Delgado. He certainly carried it off in style to become the first Spaniard to win the tour since 1973.

Previous attempts to win had not ended so happily; in 1984 he broke his collar bone in a fall, in 1986 he quit the race on learning of the death of his mother - and in 1987 he was beaten into second place by just 48 seconds, after 2,500 miles of racing! Little wonder he was pleased with his victory.

"It's compensation for a life dedicated to cycling," he gasped afterwards. "I have worked to win the Tour de France for many years."

Delgado crossed the finishing line in 84 hours, 22 minutes and 53 seconds - the hardest working, fastest moving fashion model ever!

Great gear, but no one had time to pose for a photo!

TOP 10 MUSIC VIDEOS

THIS WEEK	LAST WEEK	Title	Artist	Label
1	1	THE LEGEND CONTINUES	Michael Jackson	(Motown/VideoCollection)
2	NEW	CIAO ITALIA	Madonna	(Warner Reprise)
3	2	IF LOOKS COULD KILL	Heart	(PMI)
4	4	THE MAKING OF 'THRILLER'	Michael Jackson	(Vestron)
5	3	GLASS SPIDER VOL 2	David Bowie	(Video Collection)
6	5	VIDEO SINGLES	Wet Wet Wet	(Channel 5)
7	7	STORY TELLING	Talking Heads	(PMI)
8	8	VIEW FROM A BRIDGE	T'Pau	(Virgin)
9	10	TRILOGY	Whitesnake	(PMI)
10	14	GLASS SPIDER TOUR	David Bowie	(Video Collection)

TOP 20 ALBUMS

		Title	Artist	Label
1	8	TRACY CHAPMAN	Tracy Chapman	(Elektra)
2	1	NITELIFE	Various	(CBS)
3	2	TANGO IN THE NIGHT	Fleetwood Mac	(Warner Brothers)
4	6	PUSH	Bros	(CBS)
5	NEW	ROLL WITH IT	Steve Winwood	(Virgin)
6	10	WHITNEY HOUSTON	Whitney Houston	(Arista)
7	7	DIRTY DANCING	Soundtrack	(RCA)
8	5	HEAVEN ON EARTH	Belinda Carlisle	(Virgin)
9	NEW	IDOL SONGS - 11 OF THE BEST	Billy Idol	(Chrysalis)
10	12	STRONGER THAN PRIDE	Sade	(Epic)
11	11	POPPED IN SOULED OUT	Wet Wet Wet	(Precious Organisation)
12	4	MOTOWN DANCE PARTY	Various	(Motown)
13	3	PEOPLE	Hothouse Flowers	(London)
14	13	THE HITS OF HOUSE ARE HERE	Various	(K-Tel)
15	9	PROVISION	Scritti Politti	(Virgin)
16	17	MORE DIRTY DANCING	Various	(RCA)
17	35	BROTHERS IN ARMS	Dire Straits	(Vertigo)
18	38	ACTUALLY	Pet Shop Boys	(Parlophone)
19	NEW	LET IT BEE	Voice Of The Beehive	(London)
20	15	THE INNOCENTS	Erasure	(Mute)

TOP 10 SINGLES

WEEK 2

		Title	Artist	Label
1	2	THE TWIST (YO TWIST)	Fat Boys & Chubby Checker	(Urban)
2	13	NOTHING'S GONNA CHANGE MY LOVE FOR YOU	Glenn Medeiros	(London)
3	1	I OWE YOU NOTHING	Bros	(CBS)
4	10	PUSH IT/TRAMP	Salt 'n' Pepa	(London/Champion)
5	4	TRIBUTE (RIGHT ON)	Pasadenas	(CBS)
6	5	IN THE AIR TONIGHT '88	Phil Collins	(Virgin)
7	3	BOYS	Sabrina	(Ibiza)
8	14	FAST CAR	Tracy Chapman	(Elektra)
9	7	BREAKFAST IN BED	UB40 with Chrissie Hynde	(DEP International)
10	11	TOUGHER THAN THE REST	Bruce Springsteen	(CBS)

WEEK 3

		Title	Artist	Label
1	2	NOTHING'S GONNA CHANGE MY LOVE FOR YOU	Glenn Medeiros	(London)
2	4	PUSH IT/TRAMP	Salt 'n' Pepa	(London/Champion)
3	1	THE TWIST (YO TWIST)	Fat Boys & Chubby Checker	(Urban)
4	8	FAST CAR	Tracy Chapman	(Elektra)
5	16	ROSES ARE RED	Mac Band featuring the Mc Campbell Brothers	(MCA)
6	3	I OWE YOU NOTHING	Bros	(CBS)
7	6	IN THE AIR TONIGHT '88	Phil Collins	(Virgin)
8	39	I DON'T WANT TO TALK ABOUT IT	Everything But The Girl	(blanco y negro)
9	7	BOYS	Sabrina	(Ibiza)
10	13	WAP-BAM-BOOGIE/DON'T BLAME ME	Matt Bianco	(WEA)

WEEK 4

		Title	Artist	Label
1	1	NOTHING'S GONNA CHANGE MY LOVE FOR YOU	Glenn Medeiros	(London)
2	18	DIRTY DIANA	Michael Jackson	(Epic)
3	2	PUSH IT/TRAMP	Salt 'n' Pepa	(London/Champion)
4	8	I DON'T WANT TO TALK ABOUT IT	Everything But The Girl	(blanco y negro)
5	5	ROSES ARE RED	Mac Band featuring the Mc Campbell Brothers	(MCA)
6	4	FAST CAR	Tracy Chapman	(Elektra)
7	3	THE TWIST (YO TWIST)	Fat Boys & Chubby Checker	(Urban)
8	6	I OWE YOU NOTHING	Bros	(CBS)
9	22	MONKEY	George Michael	(Epic)
10	30	I WANT YOUR LOVE	Transvision Vamp	(MCA)

UB40

(RETNA)

In December, 1979, when Chrissie Hynde was enjoying a number one single and album in Britian, she happened to see an unknown new band playing at the legendary North London pub, The Hope and Anchor.

She liked what she heard, told the bemused players so and invited them to join The Pretenders, the hit group she sang with, on a nationwide tour. UB40 have never looked back since.

"Chrissie discovered us," says lead guitarist and singer Robin Campbell. "She gave us our big break by allowing us that important support slot at the beginning of our career. Without her, we would never have got where we are."

So it was nice when UB40 teamed up with Chrissie to record "I Got You Babe", a number one hit in 1986 - and then reformed the partnership to take the successful combination back into the Network Chart Top Ten again in July with "Breakfast In Bed". Not that UB40 really needed a helping hand any longer!

The Birmingham band's achievements over the years serve as an inspiration to every downcast person on the dole who ever dreamed about fame and fortune through music - because that's where the eight-piece multi-racial reggae outfit came from, even taking its name from the Government's dole reference form number.

Today, UB40 is very much an industry, with its own recording studios and an impressive list of chart-topping albums and singles to its credit, but the group members all still live within two miles of their original homes. They might travel around the world with their music, but where they come from is where they still want to be.

"We can operate in Birmingham," says saxophone player Brian Travers. "We're the most famous people who still live in the city, you see. Everywhere we go we get looked after - pubs stay open all night for us, we're never asked to leave. No bother, no aggro off anybody. We're the biggest fish in the pond!"

Despite their remarkable success, UB40 still manage to keep their feet on the ground – well, most of them do!

(RETNA)

AUGUST

NESCAFÉ THE NETWORK CHART SHOW

> NETWORK CHART TOP 40 <

A1	1	NOTHING'S GONNA CHANGE MY LOVE FOR YOU......Glenn Medeiros ...(London)
2	8	SUPERFLY GUY.................................S'Express.........................(Rhythm King)
3	NEW	THE LOCOMOTION.............................Kylie Minogue.............................(PWL)
4	14	THE ONLY WAY IS UP.........................Yazz & The Plastic Population.(Big Life)
5	3	I DON'T WANT TO TALK ABOUT IT......Everything But The Girl..(blanco y negro)
6	4	I WANT YOUR LOVE...........................Transvision Vamp.........................(MCA)
7	7	YOU CAME.....................................Kim Wilde..................................(MCA)
8	5	PUSH IT/TRAMP................................Salt 'n' Pepa.............(London/Champion)
9	2	DIRTY DIANA..................................Michael Jackson............................(Epic)
10	21	REACH OUT, I'LL BE THERE...............Four Tops................................(Motown)
11	10	ROSES ARE RED.....Mac Band featuring the Mc Campbell Brothers ...(MCA)
12	32	I NEED YOU..................................B.V.S.M.P................................(Debut)
13	6	FOOLISH BEAT.................................Debbie Gibson.............................(Atlantic)
14	11	LOVE BITES...................................Def Leppard.................(Bludgeon Riffola)
15	9	MONKEY..George Michael.............................(Epic)
16	53	FIND MY LOVE..................................Fairground Attraction.....................(RCA)
17	25	FEEL THE NEED IN ME.......................Shakin' Stevens...........................(Epic)
18	48	HUSTLE TO THE MUSIC...................Funky Worm................................(Fon)
19	13	THE TWIST (YO TWIST).....................Fat Boys & Chubby Checker.......(Urban)
20	20	GLAM SLAM....................................Prince................................(Paisley Park)

Siouxsie

(RETNA)

Kim Wilde

(RETNA)

21	36	PEEK A BOO.......................................Siouxsie & The Banshees ..(Wonderland)
22	12	FAST CAR..Tracy Chapman.........................(Elektra)
23	23	ALL FIRED UP......................................Pat Benatar.............................(Chrysalis)
24	18	HEAT IT UP..Wee Papa Girl Rappers.................(Jive)
25	29	WHAT CAN I SAY TO MAKE YOU LOVE ME..............Alexander O'Neal.......(Tabu)
26	16	I OWE YOU NOTHING........................Bros......................................(CBS)
27	42	I SAY NOTHING.................................Voice Of The Beehive...............(London)
28	46	MARTHA'S HARBOUR........................All About Eve.........................(Mercury)
29	15	TOMORROW PEOPLE............Ziggy Marley & The Melody Makers ......(Virgin)
30	24	I'M TOO SCARED..............................Steven Dante.........................(Chrysalis)
31	26	WAP-BAM-BOOGIE/DON'T BLAME IT ON THE GIRL........Matt Bianco ......(WEA)
32	22	BREAKFAST IN BED............UB40 with Chrissie Hynde.........(DEP International)
33	49	LIKE DREAMERS DO....Mica Paris featuring Courtney Pine ..(4th & Broadway)
34	17	FIESTA...Pogues.............................(Pogue Mahone)
35	24	BOYS..Sabrina..................................(Ibiza)
36	40	YE KE YE KE....................................Mory Kante.............................(London)
37	58	THE HARDER I TRY...........................Brother Beyond.............................(EMI)
38	60	SOMEWHERE DOWN THE CRAZY RIVER............Robbie Robertson.........(Geffen)
39	19	CROSS MY HEART..............................Eighth Wonder.............................(Epic)
40	64	HAPPY EVER AFTER..........................Julia Fordham.............................(Circa)

GLENN MEDEIROS

With its population of 1,000, the tropical Hawaiian island of Kauai was no more that a beautiful dot on the map - until Glenn Medeiros came along.

And even he was not prepared for the international impact he would have on the pop world, let alone his birthplace. Glenn scored a huge, worldwide hit with his debut single, "Nothing's Gonna Change My Love For You", and sold more than two million copies of it in the process.

He began singing in public when he was 12 years old, entertaining guests on his father's guided tours of the island.

"My father is a bus driver - most people in Hawaii work in the tourism industry," he explains. "So, when I was younger, my dad used to take me on these coach tours, and I'd sing to the passengers on board as we drove around. I used to sing them Barry Manilow songs, because at the time I was really into him, and it was great. People used to tip me all the time. Sometimes I'd make 100 dollars a day."

His talent for singing is something which Glenn says he discoverd a long time before his profitable mobile performances.

"I've always wanted to sing. Even when I was little, I used to make tapes of myself. Singing always came naturally to me, and my mum helped me a lot with my voice. She's not a professional singer, but she can sing as well as any pop singer."

Glenn's abilities proved equally impressive to judges when, at the age of 15, he entered a local talent competition - and won. Part of the prize was the opportunity to record "Nothing's Gonna Change My Love For You", which his local radio station began to give immediate airplay. Glenn was still at school when the song topped the charts in America.

"I was actually the first teenager out of the current crop of teenage singers to have a hit in the US," he proudly points out.

Today, the inevitable result has been for Glenn to emerge as the most famous resident on Kauai, but what has the reaction been from his fellow islanders?

"Well, everyone thinks it's great," he grins, "and they're behind me all the way - especially my family." The response to Glenn away from home, though just as favourable, has been of slightly more concern to him.

"I have been mobbed a few times in Europe. It's kind of scary, but I've always got guards aorund me so that girls can't touch me. I try to keep away from the fans because I think it could be quite dangerous in situations like that. But I can't understand why girls want to touch me, because I don't think I'm very good-looking."

Even so, Glenn is honest enough to admit that one of the main reasons why he began performing at all was to impress members of the opposite sex - although he never bargained on it winning him admirers all over the world. "No way. I can't believe all this has happened...!"

Glenn is happy to remain living with his family on Kauai, where he previously worked as a petrol station attendant before

(RETNA)

Glenn Medeiros – "I don't think I'm very good looking."

his singing career took off, and he's the first to make the corny pun that "nothing's gonna change my love for the island."

"The view from any part of it is lovely. Wherever you look, you can see the ocean. The sun is great, the greenery and the flowers are beautiful and, of course, we have miles of wonderful beaches. I've lived there all my life, and when you come from Kauai, it's hard not to miss it."

Watching the video for his hit single - which was filmed on location there - it's not difficult to see why.

Glenn at home on Kauai.

(RETNA)

BRINGER OF JOY

She was given an old-fashioned name meaning 'bringer of joy', and the arrival of Princess Beatrice in 1988 quickly saw her live up to it.

Her Royal Fergieness leaves hospital with her little "Beetroot".

(SYNDICATION INTERNATIONAL)

The birth of a royal baby is always a cause for national celebration, and there was certainly a carnival atmosphere outside London's Portland Hospital on August 8 when the news broke that the Duchess of York, Sarah Ferguson, had produced a healthy girl weighing 6lb 12oz at shortly after 8pm. At 9.31pm, a lone official was greeted with cheers after walking 60 yards from Buckingham Palace to post the announcement on the black iron railings - in line with tradition.

Beatrice Elizabeth Mary was delivered just over ten hours after Fergie had been admitted to hospital, and Prince Andrew was present at the birth. The latest addition to the Royal Family is the Queen's fifth grandchild - and fifth in line to the throne. She will live her life out like her parents - in the full glare of the media - and, already, astrologers have been busy looking into her future. She will, one suggests, grow up to be a very attractive but highly rebellious teenager who will probably choose to live abroad later in life and have two children.

Time will reveal all, of course, but at least one prediction concerning the new Princess looks a safe bet to actually occur - or so says David Williamson, co-editor of Debrett's Peerage, the 'top people's bible'. He is convinced there will be a boom of babies named after her.

"It will almost certainly catch on," he says. "Until she was born, I would not have expected to find anyone of that name under the age of 50 or 60, but I imagine there will soon be hundreds of little Beatrices."

They will not share the official title Her Royal Highness The Princess of York, but will inevitably find themselves being called Bea or Beatty - just like their namesake. Fergie has come up with her own nickname for her daughter to answer to. Princess Beetroot!

(SYNDICATION INTERNATIONAL)

Oops! Missed! Graham Gooch – gracious in defeat.

CATASTROPHE FOR ENGLAND'S CRICKETERS

Even coming from a man as naturally modest as Viv Richards, it must have been the understatement of the year when he reflected that his team had done the England side "a little damage."

In truth, English international cricket has rarely witnessed a more depressing or unsuccessful period in its history than the 4-0 thrashing which Richards and his players inflicted upon England last summer to take the Wisden Trophy in the Cornhill Test series. In the process, the West Indians confirmed their position as perhaps the finest cricketing force in the world, while England's already battered reputation as a team was well and truly knocked for six.

The taste of victory was even more sweet for Richards because, as a captain, he had presided over a West Indies side which had drawn its previous four Test series, and not sampled success since beating David Gower's tourists 5-0 in 1986. For England, the gruelling results which started in July and ended so dismally in August, were merely the culmination of 18 games without a win - having played every Test country barring India and Sri Lanka.

And the problems faced by England on the pitch - the summer saw four different team captains in Mike Gatting, John Emburey, Chris Cowdrey and Graham Gooch - were matched by a run of trouble off it. Gatting was sacked in disgrace over his involvement with a blonde barmaid - and then recalled for the Third Test against the West Indies - while Chris Cowdrey did his chances of re-selection little good with a public outburst in protest at his replacement as captain.

Graham Gooch, however, England's 'man of the series', managed to emerge from it all with pride. His batting average was 45.75 runs, and his highest score 146. And he was gracious in defeat.

"The West Indies were the better side, no doubt about it," he commented after the series. "They beat us out of sight in two games. It's very difficult to dominate an attack like that. I'm not saying it can't be done, but we didn't match up to it this time."

THIS WEEK	LAST WEEK			
1	1	THE LEGEND CONTINUES..	Michael Jackson	(Mowtown/Video Collection)
2	5	THE MAKING OF 'THRILLER'	Michael Jackson	(Vestron)
3	4	NOW THAT'S WHAT I CALL MUSIC 12	Various	(PMI/Virgin)
4	3	CIAO ITALIA	Madonna	(WEA)
5	2	HISTORIA	Def Leppard	(Polygram Music Video)
6	6	THE VIDEO SINGLES	Wet Wet Wet	(Channel 5)
7	15	VOLUME I	Genesis	(Virgin)
8	13	VOLUME 2	Genesis	(Virgin)
9	10	SIXTIES MIX II	Various	(Stylus)
10	8	SAVAGE	Eurythmics	(Virgin)

TOP 20 ALBUMS

1	1	NOW THAT'S WHAT I CALL MUSIC 12	Various	(EMI/Virgin/Polygram)
2	3	THE HITS ALBUM/TAPE 8	Various	(CBS/WEA/BMG)
3	2	TRACY CHAPMAN	Tracy Chapman	(Elektra)
4	5	KYLIE	Kylie Minogue	(PWL)
5	4	BAD	Michael Jackson	(Epic)
6	5	IDOL SONGS - 11 OF THE BEST	Billy Idol	(Chrysalis)
7	7	IT TAKES A NATION OF MILLIONS TO HOLD US BACK	Public Enemy	(Def Jam)
8	10	PUSH	Bros	(CBS)
9	9	TANGO IN THE NIGHT	Fleetwood Mac	(Warner Brothers)
10	12	DIRTY DANCING	Soundtrack	(RCA)
11	13	TUNNEL OF LOVE	Bruce Springsteen	(CBS)
12	NEW	FOLLOW THE LEADER	Eric B & Rakim	(MCA)
13	14	POPPED IN SOULED OUT	Wet Wet Wet	(Precious Organisation)
14	11	THE COLLECTION	Barry White	(Mercury)
15	8	SUBSTANCE 1977-1980	Joy Division	(Factory)
16	18	THRILLER	Michael Jackson	(Epic)
17	14	KICK	INXS	(Mercury)
18	18	UB40	UB40	(DEP International)
19	NEW	A SALT WITH A DEADLY PEPA	Salt 'n' Pepa	(London)
20	27	LOVE	Aztec Camera	(Warner Brothers)

TOP TO SINGLES

WEEK 2

1	4	THE ONLY WAY IS UP	Yazz & The Plastic Population	(Big Life)
2	3	THE LOCOMOTION	Kylie Minogue	(PWL)
3	12	I NEED YOU	B.V.S.M.P.	(Debut)
4	2	SUPERFLY GUY	S'Express	(Rhythm King)
5	1	NOTHING'S GONNA CHANGE MY LOVE FOR YOU	Glenn Medeiros	(London)
6	NEW	THE EVIL THAT MEN DO	Iron Maiden	(EMI)
7	7	YOU CAME	Kim Wilde	(MCA)
8	16	FIND MY LOVE	Fairground Attraction	(RCA)
9	10	REACH OUT I'LL BE THERE	Four Tops	(Motown)
10	18	HUSTLE! (TO THE MUSIC)	The Funky Worm	(Fon)

WEEK 3

1	1	THE ONLY WAY IS UP	Yazz & The Plastic Population	(Big Life)
2	2	THE LOCOMOTION	Kylie Minogue	(PWL)
3	3	I NEED YOU	B.V.S.M.P.	(Debut)
4	6	THE EVIL THAT MEN DO	Iron Maiden	(EMI)
5	4	SUPERFLY GUY	S'Express	(Rhythm King)
6	8	FIND MY LOVE	Fairground Attraction	(RCA)
7	22	HANDS TO HEAVEN	Breathe	(Siren)
8	7	YOU CAME	Kim Wilde	(MCA)
9	9	REACH OUT I'LL BE THERE	Four Tops	(Motown)
10	5	NOTHING'S GONNA CHANGE MY LOVE FOR YOU	Glenn Medeiros	(London)

WEEK 4

1	1	THE ONLY WAY IS UP	Yazz & The Plastic Population	(Big Life)
2	3	I NEED YOU	B.V.S.M.P.	(Debut)
3	7	HANDS TO HEAVEN	Breathe	(Siren)
4	2	THE LOCOMOTION	Kylie Minogue	(PWL)
5	16	THE HARDER I TRY	Brother Beyond	(EMI)
6	6	FIND MY LOVE	Fairground Attraction	(RCA)
7	14	MY LOVE	Julio Iglesias featuring Stevie Wonder	(CBS)
8	4	THE EVIL THAT MEN DO	Iron Maiden	(EMI)
9	8	YOU CAME	Kim Wilde	(MCA)
10	13	GOOD TRADITION	Tanita Tikaram	(WEA)

TOP TEN ACT

TANITA TIKARAM

Tanita Tikaram has Oxford University to thank for her sudden arrival as a successful pop singer.

Had it not been for the famous educational institution, she might have ended up a lawyer or journalist.

"Instead, after passing my 'A' Levels, I was turned down for a place at Oxford, which I got very depressed about," she says. "Then I decided I'd be a songwriter."

Naturally enough, matters were not quite so simple, especially since Tanita admits that less than two years before she had made that decision, she thought music was "really boring, and I never really listened to it."

That all changed when she chanced to hear the Joni Mitchell album, "Ladies Of The Canyon". The record was the inspiration behind Tanita making a three-track demo tape of her own compositions. Unsure of how to go about being "a world-famous singer-songwriter" herself, however, her next step was actually fairly standard.

"I thought I'd send the tape to someone," she says, "so I went out and got this music paper - I'd never read one before - to see where I should send it to. I saw an advert for the Mean Fiddler, so I sent it there."

The result was a booking at the important London venue and it was there that Tanita was discovered, on December 16, 1987, by Paul Charles, the man who is now her manager. In March, 1988, she signed to WEA Records and just 12 weeks later, her debut single "Good Tradition" was heading for the Network Chart Top Ten position it held in August. Tanita was 19 years old.

Her home town of Basingstoke had never heard a story quite like it, and neither had she. Now acclaimed as a talent mature beyond her years and a girl destined for a long and lasting career, she only has one regret.

"It's really great having a song in the charts and being in magazines along with Tiffany and Debbie Gibson," she sighs, "but I really miss my morning lie-in!"

Tanita attempts to lay a carpet with her pinky.

(RETNA)

NETWORK CHART TOP 40

1	1	*THE ONLY WAY IS UP*	**Yazz & The Plastic Population**	(Big Life)
2	5	*THE HARDER I TRY*	**Brother Beyond**	(EMI)
3	7	*MY LOVE*	**Julio Iglesias featuring Stevie Wonder**	(CBS)
4	3	*HANDS TO HEAVEN*	**Breathe**	(Siren)
5	4	*THE LOCOMOTION*	**Kylie Minogue**	(PWL)
6	6	*FIND MY LOVE*	**Fairground Attraction**	(RCA)
7	2	*I NEED YOU*	**B.V.S.M.P.**	(Debut)
8	23	*DON'T MAKE ME WAIT/MEGABLAST*	**Bomb The Bass**	(Rhythm King)
9	10	*GOOD TRADITION*	**Tanita Tikaram**	(WEA)
10	2	*ON THE BEACH SUMMER '88*	**Chris Rea**	(WEA)
11	17	*SOMEWHERE DOWN THE CRAZY RIVER*	**Robbie Robertson**	(Geffen)
12	27	*TEARDROPS*	**Womack & Womack**	(4th & Broadway)
13	16	*KING OF EMOTION*	**Big Country**	(Mercury)
14	42	*THE RACE*	**Yello**	(Mercury)
15	44	*TOUCHY*	**A-ha**	(Warner Brothers)
16	20	*SWEET CHILD O' MINE*	**Guns 'N' Roses**	(Geffen)
17	6	*YOU CAME*	**Kim Wilde**	(MCA)
18	19	*RUNNING ALL OVER THE WORLD*	**Status Quo**	(Vertigo)
19	NEw	*A GROOVY KIND OF LOVE*	**Phil Collins**	(Virgin)
20	21	*ANYTHING FOR YOU*	**Gloria Estefan**	(Epic)
21	29	*RUSH HOUR*	**Jane Wiedlin**	(EMI Manhattan)
22	8	*THE EVIL THAT MEN DO*	**Iron Maiden**	(EMI)
23	25	*YE KE YE KE*	**Mory Kante**	(London)
24	13	*SUPERFLY GUY*	**S'Express**	(Rhythm King)
25	11	*MARTHA'S HARBOUR*	**All About Eve**	(Mercury)
26	39	*EVERY GIRL & BOY*	**Spagna**	(CBS)
27	NEw	*HARVESTER OF SORROW*	**Metallica**	(Vertigo)
28	32	*SUPERSTITIOUS*	**Europe**	(CBS)
29	14	*HUSTLE! TO THE MUSIC*	**Funky Worm**	(Fon)
30	37	*SOLDIER OF LOVE*	**Donny Osmond**	(Virgin)
31	15	*REACH OUT I'LL BE THERE*	**Four Tops**	(Motown)
32	22	*WHEN IT'S LOVE*	**Van Halen**	(Warner Brothers)
33	34	*I WON'T BLEED FOR YOU*	**Climie Fisher**	(EMI)
34	41	*WHERE DID I GO WRONG*	**UB40**	(DEP International)
35	30	*JUMP START*	**Natalie Cole**	(Manhattan)
36	69	*I'M GOING TO BE (500 MILES)*	**Proclaimers**	(Chrysalis)
37	72	*HE AIN'T HEAVY HE'S MY BROTHER*	**Bill Medley**	(Polydor)
38	NEW	*HEAVEN IN MY HANDS*	**Level 42**	(Polydor)
39	40	*EASY*	**Commodores**	(Motown)
40	NEW	*WAY BEHIND ME*	**Primitives**	(Lazy)

Brother Beyond

(RETNA)

YAZZ

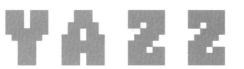

Getting to number one in the charts affects different people in different ways.

Some reach for the champagne, others feel a sudden urge to leap wildly into the air, and at least one singer - Feargal Sharkey - was moved to grab the nearest London telephone directory, pick a number at random and ring it up to spread the good news. Yazz simply burst into tears.

Her debut solo single, "The Only Way Is Up", was one of the surprise hits of the year, and also the biggest selling of '88, staying on top for five weeks. But when the record first arrived in the pole position, it all proved too much for Yazz.

"I just cried," she says, remembering the moment. "I cried my eyes out. I even cried before I sang the song on Top of the Pops."

Perhaps more than anything, the 28-year-old singer was weeping with relief. Years of struggling to make it in the music business had finally paid off for her. Her string of previous jobs had certainly always been a means to an end.

"When I left school I worked in the claims and insurance department of London Transport, and I got fired," she says. "Then I got a job at the Post Office - and I got fired. I worked in loads of shops and as a waitress in a nightclub, but I always just wanted to be a musician. I did some awful work, but I knew 9 to 5 wasn't for me."

It was while working at the nightclub that Yazz began to see a way of avoiding all that.

"I started to fall in love with dance music, and also to meet people in bands," she recalls. "The first proper band I got involved with I was playing keyboards, and then one day the singer didn't turn up. So I started singing instead, and decided I quite enjoyed it. The band had an embarrassing name - I can't really remember

(RETNA)

Yasmin Evans – Yazz to her pals.

it, actually. The Flowers... something to do with flowers, but that group folded after a while. We did about one concert and that was it."

Other former occupations for Yazz have included being a successful fashion model and, more recently, a clothes stylist for clients including Pepsi and Shirlie, Nik Kershaw - and George Michael.

"I worked for George at a time when I didn't have much money, and it turned out to be a really good thing to do. He's so cool, and very easy to work with. He's very nice, very polite and very warm. I got all the clothes together for the Wham! tours. I had the same management and, because I knew designers from my modelling days, George asked me to help."

Her modelling days came to an abrupt end when Yazz dramatically altered the way she looked.

"About four years ago, I cut all my hair off and decided to go the whole way and bleach it too. I thought it would go brassy - but it went really bright blonde. I never got another modelling job after that! I did catwalk modelling, that sort of thing - but mainly for the money so I could afford musical instruments and studio time. But it was good fun."

Yazz, real name Yasmin Evans, first made a musical impression on the charts as the singer on "Doctorin' The House", a Top Ten hit for Coldcut, and is perfectly happy that her days on the catwalk are behind her now - however much she enjoyed them at the time.

"But I'd hate people to think I was another model turned singer," she admits. "I'm a real singer who just happened to be a model."

Her chart-topping success was all the more important to Yazz because it was with a song that very much mirrored her own life.

"'The Only Way Is Up' is about being on the dole and down and out, but not worrying about it," she explains. "It concerns keeping on doing what you want to do, because you can get through in the end. It's exactly what I've done to get where I am now and, like the song says, the only way is up!"

(RETNA)

HURRICANE SAVAGES CARIBBEAN

Buildings were blown down, planes were tossed like toys through the air, trees felled as if they were matchsticks - and scores of people lost their lives in the world's worst storm of the century.

When Hurricane Gilbert struck the Caribbean in September, anything in its path was swept aside without mercy by raging winds of up to 200 miles per hour. And with the vicious gales came torrents of rain which in turn caused floods that led to a further loss of life. Worst hit by Gilbert was the beautiful island of Jamaica, where the eye of the hurricane caused enormous devastation and damage estimated at $4 billion.

It left more than 500,000 people without a home and, in declaring a state of emergency, the Jamaican Prime Minister Edward Seaga likened the wreckage to "Hiroshima after the atom bomb." It was an appropriate comparison - Gilbert contained energy equivalent to several million times the world's entire nuclear arsenal!

From Jamaica, the 500-mile-wide storm moved on through the Caribbean and roared toward the Gulf of Mexico, where thousands of residents had fled their homes to seek refuge away from its fury. Huge waves broke in the streets of coastal towns in Texas, washing ships ashore into houses, and with its last tragic blow Hurricane Gilbert swept more than 200 people to their deaths in rising floods as they sought safety in coaches leaving the area.

The hurricane finally blew itself out in the hills below Monterrey - where another 60 victims were claimed in flash floods, and 200,000 homeless survivors helplessly surveyed the massive damage to property and valuable crops.

In the aftermath of the disaster, the rebuilding of lives, land and homes continues, perhaps with the words of one Methodist minister still ringing in people's minds. "In God we trust," he wrote outside his abandoned church. "Gilbert is another story. Goodbye..."

(ASSOCIATED PRESS)

Pilotless parked planes embarked on unscheduled flights when Gilbert arrived.

THE SHAME AND THE GLORY

When sport ceases to be fair, it stops being sport - and when spectators can no longer believe what they see, why bother watching at all?

Such were the topics under discussion following the Games of the XXIV Olympiad in Seoul. The 1988 Olympics, like any other which had gone before them, will be remembered for the triumphs, the heartaches, the winning and the losing but, for all time, they will be remembered for the controversy surrounding the use of drugs by athletes and for one of the stars who fell from grace - Ben Johnson.

He succeeded in becoming the fastest man on earth - having run the 100 metres sprint in a world record 9.79 seconds - and then brought his life and career tumbling down after illegal substances were found in his urine samples. The discovery, and Johnson's subsequent return home to Canada in disgrace having been stripped of his gold medal, was undoubtedly the story of the Games.

Fortunately, there were other, more inspiring tales to be told by the time the Olympic flame had finally been extinguished - particularly from among the 24 British medalists. There were golds for Adrian Moorhouse in the 100 metre breaststroke, Malcolm Cooper in shooting, Andy Holmes and Steve Redgrave in rowing, Mike McIntyre and Bryn Vaile in yachting and for the men's hockey team. Other notable British results included sprinter Linford Christie's two silver medals - in the 100 metre and 4 x 100 metre relay races, but Fatima Whitbread had to be content with silver in javelin. Daley Thompson failed valiantly in his attempt at a third gold in the decathlon and he, like Steve Cram, surprisingly came away without a medal at all.

Not so Florence Griffith-Joyner. She collected three golds, one silver and two world records in the 100 and 200 metre events. But neither her achievements nor those of any other competitor can alter the fact that the Seoul Olympics will forever be remembered by another title. The Ben Johnson Games.

Johnson, Christie and Lewis in the men's 100m final.

(ALLSPORT)

THIS WEEK
LAST WEEK

TOP 10 MUSIC VIDEOS

This Week	Last Week	Title	Artist	Label
1	1	THE LEGEND CONTINUES	Michael Jackson	(Motown/Video Collection)
2	2	CIAO ITALIA	Madonna	(Warner Reprise)
3	3	HISTORIA	Def Leppard	(Bludgeon Riffola)
4	7	KICK FLICK	INXS	(Vestron)
5	4	THE MAKING OF 'THRILLER'	Michael Jackson	(Vestron)
6	5	VIDEOS VOLUME 1	Genesis	(Virgin)
7	6	VIDEOS VOLUME 2	Genesis	(Virgin)
8	9	SINGLES	Wet Wet Wet	(Channel 5)
9	NEW	LIVE	Prince	(Channel 5)
10	8	IF LOOKS COULD KILL	Heart	(PMI)

TOP 20 ALBUMS

This Week	Last Week	Title	Artist	Label
1	3	THE FIRST OF A MILLION KISSES	Fairground Attraction	(RCA)
2	2	KYLIE	Kylie Minogue	(PWL)
3	4	TRACY CHAPMAN	Tracy Chapman	(Elektra)
4	1	NOW THAT'S WHAT I CALL MUSIC 12	Various	(EMI/Virgin/Polygram)
5	7	THE GREATEST EVER ROCK 'N' ROLL MIX	Various	(Stylus)
6	6	THE BEST OF THE EAGLES	Eagles	(Asylum)
7	5	IDOL SONGS - 11 OF THE BEST	Billy Idol	(Chrysalis)
8	10	TURN BACK THE CLOCK	Johnny Hates Jazz	(Virgin)
9	9	BAD	Michael Jackson	(Epic)
10	11	DIRTY DANCING	Soundtrack	(RCA)
11	38	HOT CITY NIGHTS	Various	(Vertigo)
12	8	THE HITS ALBUM/TAPE 8	Various	(CBS/WEA/BMG)
13	13	HYSTERIA	Def Leppard	(Bludgeon Riffola)
14	12	TANGO IN THE NIGHT	Fleetwood Mac	(Warner Brothers)
15	41	ROBBIE ROBERTSON	Robbie Robertson	(Geffen)
16	16	KICK	INXS	(Mercury)
17	NEW	SO GOOD	Mica Paris	(4th & Broadway)
18	17	LOVE	Aztec Camera	(Warner Brothers)
19	19	THE COLLECTION	Barry White	(Mercury)
20	14	ROCK THE WORLD	5 Star	(Tent)

TOP 10 SINGLES

WEEK 2

This Week	Last Week	Title	Artist	Label
1	1	THE ONLY WAY IS UP	Yazz & The Plastic Population	(Big Life)
2	2	THE HARDER I TRY	Brother Beyond	(EMI)
3	19	A GROOVY KIND OF LOVE	Phil Collins	(Virgin)
4	12	TEARDROPS	Womack & Womack	(4th & Broadway)
5	8	DON'T MAKE ME WAIT/MEGABLAST	Bomb The Bass	(Rhythm King)
6	14	THE RACE	Yello	(Mercury)
7	3	MY LOVE	Julio Iglesias featuring Stevie Wonder	(CBS)
8	4	HANDS TO HEAVEN	Breathe	(Siren)
9	47	HE AIN'T HEAVY HE'S MY BROTHER	The Hollies	(EMI)
10	38	HEAVEN IN MY HANDS	Level 42	(Polydor)

WEEK 3

This Week	Last Week	Title	Artist	Label
1	9	HE AIN'T HEAVY HE'S MY BROTHER	The Hollies	(EMI)
2	3	A GROOVY KIND OF LOVE	Phil Collins	(Virgin)
3	4	TEARDROPS	Womack & Womack	(4th & Broadway)
4	6	THE RACE	Yello	(Mercury)
5	1	THE ONLY WAY IS UP	Yazz & The Plastic Population	(Big Life)
6	2	THE HARDER I TRY	Brother Beyond	(EMI)
7	36	LOVELY DAY (SUNSHINE MIX)	Bill Withers	(CBS)
8	NEW	I QUIT	Bros	(CBS)
9	5	DON'T MAKE ME WAIT/MEGABLAST	Bomb The Bass	(Rhythm King)
10	1	HEAVEN IN MY HANDS	Level 42	(Polydor)

WEEK 4

This Week	Last Week	Title	Artist	Label
1	1	HE AIN'T HEAVY HE'S MY BROTHER	The Hollies	(EMI)
2	2	A GROOVY KIND OF LOVE	Phil Collins	(Virgin)
3	8	I QUIT	Bros	(CBS)
4	7	LOVELY DAY (SUNSHINE MIX)	Bill Withers	(CBS)
5	3	TEARDROPS	Womack & Womack	(4th & Broadway)
6	20	NOTHING CAN DIVIDE US	Jason Donovan	(PWL)
7	NEW	DOMINO DANCING	Pet Shop Boys	(Parlophone)
8	4	THE RACE	Yello	(Mercury)
9	6	THE HARDER I TRY	Brother Beyond	(Parlophone)
10	15	EASY	The Commodores	(Motown)

OCTOBER

NESCAFÉ THE NETWORK CHART SHOW

NETWORK CHART TOP 40

1	1	*HE AIN'T HEAVY HE'S MY BROTHER*	**The Hollies**	(EMI)
2	4	*LOVELY DAY (SUNSHINE MIX)*	**Bill Withers**	(CBS)
3	2	*A GROOVY KIND OF LOVE*	**Phil Collins**	(Virgin)
4	NEW	*DESIRE*	**U2**	(Island)
5	7	*DOMINO DANCING*	**Pet Shop Boys**	(Parlophone)
6	6	*NOTHING CAN DIVIDE US*	**Jason Donovan**	(PWL)
7	5	*TEARDROPS*	**Womack & Womack**	(4th & Broadway)
8	13	*BIG FUN*	**Inner City featuring Kevin Saunderson**	(10)
9	21	*SHE WANTS TO DANCE WITH ME*	**Rick Astley**	(RCA)
10	8	*THE RACE*	**Yello**	(Mercury)
11	3	*I QUIT*	**Bros**	(CBS)
12	15	*RIDING ON A TRAIN*	**Pasadenas**	(CBS)
13	25	*ONE MOMENT IN TIME*	**Whitney Houston**	(Arista)
14	22	*BAD MEDICINE*	**Bon Jovi**	(Vertigo)
15	11	*ANYTHING FOR YOU*	**Gloria Estefan & The Miami Sound Machine**	(Epic)
16	12	*THE ONLY WAY IS UP*	**Yazz & The Plastic Population**	(Big Life)
17	18	*STOP THIS CRAZY THING*	**Coldcut featuring Junior Reid**	(Ahead Of Our Time)
18	14	*I'M GONNA BE (500 MILES)*	**Proclaimers**	(Chrysalis)
19	10	*EASY*	**The Commodores**	(Motown)
20	20	*SHAKE YOUR THANG (IT'S YOUR THING)*	**Salt 'n' Pepa**	(London)

Bananarama

(LONDON)

(ARISTA)

Whitney Houston

21	40	*LOVE, TRUTH & HONESTY*	**Bananarama**	(London)
22	9	*THE HARDER I TRY*	**Brother Beyond**	(EMI)
23	37	*FAKE '88*	**Alexander O'Neal**	(Tabu)
24	16	*MEGABLAST*	**Bomb The Bass**	(Rhythm King)
25	28	*WORLD WITHOUT YOU*	**Belinda Carlisle**	(Virgin)
26	50	*TURN IT INTO LOVE*	**Hazell Dean**	(EMI)
27	29	*BURN IT UP*	**Beatmasters featuring P.P. Arnold**	(Rhythm King)
28	32	*REVOLUTION BABY*	**Transvision Vamp**	(MCA)
29	17	*ANOTHER PART OF ME*	**Michael Jackson**	(Epic)
30	47	*SPARE PARTS*	**Bruce Springsteen**	(CBS)
31	19	*RUSH HOUSE*	**Jane Wiedlin**	(EMI Manhattan)
32	62	*IT'S YER MONEY I'M AFTER BABY*	**Wonder Stuff**	(Polydor)
33	59	*I DON'T BELIEVE IN MIRACLES*	**Sinitta**	(Fanfare)
34	NEW	*A LITTLE RESPECT*	**Erasure**	(Mute)
35	23	*MY LOVE*	**Julio Iglesias**	(CBS)
36	NEW	*SECRET GARDEN*	**T'Pau**	(Siren)
37	24	*HANDS TO HEAVEN*	**Breathe**	(Siren)
38	33	*EVERY GIRL & BOY*	**Spagna**	(CBS)
39	NEW	*I DON'T WANT YOUR LOVE*	**Duran Duran**	(EMI)
40	27	*TEARS RUN RINGS*	**Marc Almond**	(Parlophone)

THE HOLLIES

OCTOBER NUMBER 1 ONE ACT

Tiffany, Bros, Debbie Gibson, Kylie Minogue, Tanita Tikaram... none of them were even born when The Hollies started having hits.

That's just part of the reason why the group was so surprised to find itself back in business with a major Networt Chart number one in October - but even more astonishing to all concerned was the fact that the song which put them there was originally a hit 19 years ago. And when "He Ain't Heavy He's My Brother" was first released in 1969, it stopped short of the top spot at number three.

The unexpected revival of the group's career was brought about by a happy 'accident' which has also resurrected the fortunes of everyone from Jackie Wilson, Percy Sledge and Ben E. King in recent years - the power of advertising. "He Ain't Heavy He's My Brother" was selected as the theme tune to a TV commercial for Miller Lite beer, and re-released when viewers - many of whom were young enough never to have heard it before - began taking a real shine to the song.

Allan Clarke, lead singer with The Hollies, is not particularly bothered about the reasons for the classic record winning new interest. He's simply amazed that it happened at all. It put the group back in the charts for the first time in seven years. Their last hit, a Hollies medley called Holliedaze, made the Top 30 in 1981.

"If somebody had told me a few months before "He Ain't Heavy He's My Brother" reached number one that it was going to get there, I wouldn't have believed them," he admits. "After all these years, it's almost unbelievable that we've got another hit to our credit. To be honest, I would have settled for it just making the Top Ten - that was amazing enough in itself - but to go all the way... well, that was just incredible!"

Allan, 46 - old enough to be the father of many of the other Network Chart acts - was most satisfied with the hit because it proved that a good song will never go out of fashion.

"It's not just the older people who are listening to our music," he says. "A lot of younger people who missed it the first time around sing along to it, too. And it was great to be back on Top of the Pops again - especially at my age! It goes to prove that there is no age limit in the music business now."

The Hollies celebrated their 25th anniversary together in 1988, and though only three of the original members are still in the group - Allan, guitarist Tony Hicks and drummer Bobby Elliott - there has been little let-up in popularity for them since the beginning. That might not be obvious from looking at the charts in recent years, but The Hollies have never stopped working. After all, there are a lot of hits to play; 22 Top 20 smashes between 1963 and 1974, including their first and only other number one - "I'm Alive", from 1965.

"Everyone in pop always talks about the good old days of the Sixties," says Bobby, "but things are better for us now than they were then!" Tony agrees. "We've never stopped touring. In an average year we tour Australia, New Zealand, Canada, America, Germany, Scandinavia and Britain. And we still do all the old hits when we play live. We know exactly what people want from us, but we try to approach the songs differently or it would get pretty boring - for everyone."

Bobby is keen to impress that the latest success of "He Ain't Heavy" was not a comeback for The Hollies - "because we've never been away" - but Allan happily owns up to being stumped by the situation for all that. Neither is he making any guesses about how long the 'revival' will last.

"I thought we would be a flash in the pan in the Sixties," he shrugs, "and look what happened..."

(RETNA)

MERCY MISSION SAVES WHALE

The drama unfolded at the roof of the globe and brought its two super powers together as millions followed their every move.

The quite extraordinary operation to lead three helpless whales to freedom after they became trapped under the ice in the wilderness of the Arctic captured the sympathy and imagination of

Eskimos look on helplessly as a stranded whale flounders in the icy water.

(COLOURIFIC)

the world. It all began on October 7 when Eskimos discovered the whales battering against the ice in a bid to reach open air, and rapidly escalated into an international incident. The plight of the gentle giants, nicknamed Crossbeak, Bonnet and Bone, spread like wildfire after the news first broke in the small Alaskan outpost of Barrow, population 3,400.

Within days, a large team of volunteers had assembled at the northernmost point in the United States to help clear the way to the open Beaufort Sea and set the whales free. Work to achieve that started simply enough, with Eskimos using chainsaws, picks and axes to cut breathing holes in the ice, but it was soon stepped up into an elaborate, full-scale rescue plan. Ultimately, it would cost more than $1 million, and unite the East and West in an unbelievable combined mission.

From the Russians came the ice-breaking ship Vladimir Arseniev, and from the Americans a whole battery of expensive equipment - including helicopters and a cargo plane - which all helped to find a way out of the icy prison. The exhausting battle to survive eventually killed the youngest whale, Bone, but after three weeks of a touching joint effort, Crossbeak and Bonnet finally followed in the wake of the Russian craft to escape.

Whether or not the battered and bruised creatures ever lived to tell the tale of how man saved their lives is impossible to establish. Scientists involved in the mercy mission decided not to attach radio transmitters to chart their progress mainly because the devices would only add to the whales' distress.

DAVIS SAVAGES HURRICANE

Steve Davis hits a ball with a stick.

(SYNDICATION INTERNATIONAL)

As Steve Davis has often remarked, all he does is put balls in holes with a stick, but nobody does it better or with more clinical precision.

That's why he has become a millionaire from playing snooker, why so many people consider him a boring, emotionless machine - and why the merest threat of him being trounced by the wayward skills of Alex Higgins has always proved such a popular attraction in the game.

So it was, once again, when Steve 'Interesting' Davis - with five World titles to his credit - faced the self-styled 'People's Champion' in the final of the Rothmans Grand Prix tournament during October. For Davis it perhaps signified little more than another opportunity to add to his already brimming trophy cabinet and bank balance. For Higgins it was an important chance to

prove that he could still challenge at the highest level. In his first major semi-final for two years, and having slipped out of the top 16 world rankings, he believed he was capable, and warned "I can do things with a cue."

In the event, he could never do enough and Davis romped home to take the final by 10 frames to 6 - and pocket the £65,000 winner's cheque. Traditionally, there has been little love lost between the two players whose styles and personalities are poles apart, but in his moment of triumph Davis took the microphone and spoke a few simple words in tribute to his naturally brilliant if troubled opponent. "It takes a great champion and a great character to come back," he said.

Higgins, who by then had lost to Davis 22 times in 26 encounters, took defeat like a gentleman and faced the fact that his best days might now be behind him.

"I'm not sure the Hurricane will ever blow again at Force 10," he shrugged, "but there's no point in hating someone just because he's maybe beaten you 20 times in a row. It's only a game..."

TOP 10 MUSIC VIDEOS

	THIS WEEK	LAST WEEK	Title	Artist	Label
	1	1	THE LEGEND CONTINUES	Michael Jackson	(Motown/Video Collection)
	2	NEW	TANGO IN THE NIGHT	Fleetwood Mac	(Warner)
	3	3	CIAO ITALIA	Madonna	(Warner Reprise)
	4	5	THE MAKING OF 'THRILLER'	Michael Jackson	(Vestron)
	5	2	HISTORIA	Def Leppard	(Bludgeon Riffola)
	6	7	KICK FLICK	INXS	(Channel 5)
	7	6	LIVE	Prince	(Channel 5)
	8	8	EVERYTHING	Climie Fisher	(PMI)
	9	4	CRAZY NIGHTS	Kiss	(Channel 5)
	10	10	SINGLES	Wet Wet Wet	(Channel 5)

TOP 20 ALBUMS

		Title	Artist	Label
1	NEW	STARING AT THE SUN	Level 42	(Polydor)
2	NEW	NEW JERSEY	Bon Jovi	(Vertigo)
3	2	HOT CITY NIGHTS	Various	(Vertigo)
4	1	KYLIE	Kylie Minogue	(PWL)
5	8	BAD	Michael Jackson	(Epic)
6	3	RAP TRAX!	Various	(Stylus)
7	5	TRACY CHAPMAN	Tracy Chapman	(Elektra)
8	17	BUSTER - ORIGINAL SOUNDTRACK	Various	(Virgin)
9	19	CONSCIENCE	Womack & Womack	(4th & Broadway)
10	7	THE FIRST OF A MILLION KISSES	Fairground Attraction	(RCA)
11	6	PUSH	Bros	(CBS)
12	29	SUNSHINE ON LEITH	Proclaimers	(Chrysalis)
13	10	NOW THAT'S WHAT I CALL MUSIC 12	Various	(EMI/Virgin/Polygram)
14	42	ANCIENT HEART	Tanita Tikaram	(WEA)
15	15	DIRTY DANCING	Soundtrack	(RCA)
16	4	RANK	The Smiths	(Rough Trade)
17	NEW	BLUE BELL KNOLL	Cocteau Twins	(4AD)
18	22	SPIRIT OF EDEN	Talk Talk	(Parlophone)
19	11	THE GREATEST EVER ROCK 'N' ROLL MIX	Various	(Stylus)
20	27	WHITNEY	Whitney Houston	(Arista)

TOP 10 SINGLES

WEEK 2

		Title	Artist	Label
1	4	DESIRE	U2	(Island)
2	1	HE AIN'T HEAVY HE'S MY BROTHER	The Hollies	(EMI)
3	13	ONE MOMENT IN TIME	Whitney Houston	(Arista)
4	5	DOMINO DANCING	Pet Shop Boys	(Parlophone)
5	3	A GROOVY KIND OF LOVE	Phil Collins	(Virgin)
6	2	LOVELY DAY (SUNSHINE MIX)	Bill Withers	(CBS)
7	44	DON'T WORRY BE HAPPY	Bobby McFerrin	(EMI Manhattan)
8	9	SHE WANTS TO DANCE WITH ME	Rick Astley	(RCA)
9	8	BIG FUN	Inner City featuring Kevin Saunderson	(10)
10	34	A LITTLE RESPECT	Erasure	(Mute)

WEEK 3

		Title	Artist	Label
1	1	DESIRE	U2	(Island)
2	3	ONE MOMENT IN TIME	Whitney Houston	(Arista)
3	7	DON'T WORRY BE HAPPY	Bobby McFerrin	(EMI Manhattan)
4	2	HE AIN'T HEAVY HE'S MY BROTHER	The Hollies	(EMI)
5	8	SHE WANTS TO DANCE WITH ME	Rick Astley	(RCA)
6	10	A LITTLE RESPECT	Erasure	(Mute)
7	5	A GROOVY KIND OF LOVE	Phil Collins	(Virgin)
8	4	DOMINO DANCING	Pet Shop Boys	(Parlophone)
9	2	WEE RULE	Wee Papa Girl Rappers	(Jive)
10	9	BIG FUN	Inner City featuring Kevin Saunderson	(10)

WEEK 4

		Title	Artist	Label
1	2	ONE MOMENT IN TIME	Whitney Houston	(Arista)
2	3	DON'T WORRY BE HAPPY	Bobby McFerrin	(EMI Manhattan)
3	9	WEE RULE	Wee Papa Girl Rappers	(Jive)
4	6	A LITTLE RESPECT	Erasure	(Mute)
5	1	DESIRE	U2	(Island)
6	42	WE CALL IT ACIEED	D. Mob	(London)
7	5	SHE WANTS TO DANCE WITH ME	Rick Astley	(RCA)
8	22	BURN IT UP	Beatmasters featuring P.P. Arnold	(Rhythm King)
9	26	HARVEST FOR THE WORLD	The Christians	(Island)
10	10	ORINOCO FLOW (SAIL AWAY)	Enya	(WEA)

TOP TEN ACT
RICK ASTLEY

Rick Astley is not one to shout about success. Following a string of international hits (his first, "Never Gonna Give You Up", reached number one in the UK, US and 14 other countries) he still sees himself as little more than someone who "just does a bit of singing."

But after making the Network Chart Top Ten in October with "She Wants To Dance With Me", he did allow himself a rare pat on the back, and even a few proud words to go with it. All but one of his previous hits had been songs penned by the winning talents of Stock, Aitken and Waterman, Rick wrote this hit himself.

"I wrote it and co-produced it, actually," he grins, "and it was very important to me that it did well so I could prove people wrong about not being able to do things on my own."

Rick was no more than a hopeful young boy from Newton-le-Willows - right in the middle of Warrington, St. Helens, Wigan and Leigh - when he was discovered singing in a local nightclub by Peter Waterman and invited down to London to start building a career with the SAW partnership. At the time he was working in his father's garden centre.

"For two years after I agreed to work with Pete, I wasn't allowed to make a single," he recalls. "They thought I was too timid, so I started off as a teaboy in the studio. Doing that gave me the confidence to meet people."

At the same time, Rick was encouraged to get to know his way around the studio and obviously picked up a lot of useful tips that would prove invaluable when he eventually came to try his hand at the mixing desk with "She Wants To Dance With Me". Not that Rick is the kind of pop star to let his talents go to his head.

"I'm just a young lad from a small town," says the international superstar!

Rick worked his way out of the garden centre, into the tea room and then into the charts!

NOVEMBER

NESCAFÉ THE NETWORK CHART SHOW

▶ NETWORK CHART TOP 40 ◀

1	2	ORINOCO FLOW (SAIL AWAY)........Enya ....(WEA)
2	5	JE NE SAIS PAS POURQUOI ....Kylie Minogue ....(PWL)
3	17	STAND UP FOR YOUR LOVE RIGHTS........Yazz & The Plastic Population ....(Big Life)
4	1	WE CALL IT ACIEED.......................D. Mob ....(London)
5	40	KISS.....................Art Of Noise featuring Tom Jones ....(China)
6	10	GIRL YOU KNOW IT'S TRUE ....Milli Vanilli ....(Cooltempo)
7	4	HARVEST FOR THE WORLD............The Christians ....(Island)
8	21	SHE MAKES MY DAY.....................Robert Palmer ....(EMI)
9	7	A LITTLE RESPECT ....Erasure ....(Mute)
10	3	ONE MOMENT IN TIME.................Whitney Houston ....(Arista)
11	13	CAN YOU PARTY..........................Royal House ....(Champion)
12	6	DON'T WORRY BE HAPPY ....Bobby McFerrin ....(EMI Manhattan)
13	15	REAL GONE KID ....Deacon Blue ....(CBS)
14	11	BURN IT UP....................Beatmasters featuring P.P. Arnold............(Rhythm King)
15	9	WEE RULE..................................Wee Papa Girl Rappers ....(Jive)
16	9	I'LL HOUSE YOU............................Richie Rich meets Jungle Brothers _(Gee Street)
17	14	TEARDROPS...............................Womack & Womack...................(4th & Broadway)
18	8	NEVER TRUST A STRANGER...........Kim Wilde ....(MCA)
19	37	THE FIRST TIME.......................Robin Beck ....(Mercury)
20	22	TWIST IN MY SOBRIETY................Tanita Tikaram ....(WEA)
21	39	1-2-3.................Gloria Estefan & The Miami Sound Machine.....................(Epic)
22	12	SHE WANTS TO DANCE WITH ME..Rick Astley..............................(RCA)
23	25	ACID MAN.................................Jolly Rodger ....(10)
24	27	THE PARTY.................................Kraze ....(MCA)
25	33	WELCOME TO THE JUNGLE/NIGHT TRAIN....... Guns 'N' Roses ....(Geffen)
26	24	BIG FUN.................................Inner City featuring Kevin Saunderson........(10)
27	44	TAKE A LOOK ....Level 42 ....(Polydor)
28	20	A GROOVY KIND OF LOVE.............Phil Collins ....(Virgin)
29	NEW	I WISH U HEAVEN.........................Prince ....(Paisley Park)
30	16	HE AIN'T HEAVY HE'S MY BROTHER..................The Hollies ....(EMI)
31	36	NOTHIN' AT ALL..........................Heart....................................(Capital)
32	NEW	LET'S STICK TOGETHER................Bryan Ferry ....(E.G.)
33	18	DESIRE.................................U2...(Island)
34	28	NOTHING CAN DIVIDE US.............Jason Donovan ....(PWL)
35	NEW	HERE COMES THAT SOUND..........Simon Harris ....(London)
36	41	LOVE IS ALL THAT MATTERS ....Human League ....(Virgin)
37	23	SECRET GARDEN.........................T'Pau ....(Siren)
38	NEW	SHARP AS A KNIFE.......Brandon Cooke featuring Roxanne Shante.............(Club)
39	NEW	HE AIN'T NO COMPETITION..........Brother Beyond ....(Parlophone)
40	42	BREATHE LIFE INTO ME.................Mica Paris ....(4th & Broadway)

(RETNA)

Tom Jones

Deacon Blue

(RETNA)

E
N
Y
A

Where Enya comes from, "there is no such thing as time." Only the lush valleys, coastal cliffs and blissful peace of a village in the north-west of Ireland which has hardly changed in centuries. In Gweedore, life goes on as it always has.

"It's really wild because of the weather," the 27-year-old singer explains. "It's always raining. Everything is green and fresh and so quiet. Perhaps because of that, everyone is very laid back. Gweedore is one of those places where all the women get married and have lots of children."

Pop music does not feature highly on the list of priorities for any of its relaxed inhabitants - and neither had it meant a thing to Enya until last September. Just like her sleepy birthplace, she is clearly as different from the norm as the gentle, choral melodies she crafted on the Network Chart 's most unusual number one of the year - "Orinoco Flow". Not for her a youth spent beside the radio or intently looking out for her favourite idols on TV...

"When my song got to the top, I was asked 'What was the first single you ever bought?'" she recalls, "and I thought 'I have never bought a single or an album. Even as a teenager!' It's strange - I don't like listening to music! People find it hard to understand that."

Instead, Enya spends any spare time she has without even people, let alone music, in earshot.

"I like to spend time on my own," she says. "I like to just sit in the quiet. Sometimes I go outside, see ordinary people with nine- to-five jobs and I'm envious. At other times I just think 'Oh, God help them!'"

Christened Eithne Ni Bhraonain - Enya is the phonetic spelling of her Gaelic first name - she comes from a large family which has a musical background spanning generations. Her mother is a music teacher, her father once played in a group called the Slieve Foy Dance Band - and three out of her four brothers and four sisters have also tasted chart success before her.

Maire, Kieran and Paul - along with two of Enya's uncles - are famous for being part of Clannad, whose most notable hit to date was "Harry's Game". Enya spent a spell with the group herself, and her keyboard contributions during that time played an influential part in its distinctive, haunting style.

Music has always haunted Enya and she has never seriously considered doing anything else in her life.

"I left school when I was 17 and went straight into studying music at college," she explains. "After a year of that, I started touring with Clannad - so I never had a regular job."

She left Clannad at the same time as manager Nicky Ryan and his wife Roma, and originally the three had plans for forming another group together. Instead, Enya lived with the Ryans in Dublin for six years - a period which found her composing and practising the music from which her solo career was to develop. Her first major break came in 1985, when director David Puttnam commissioned her to write the score for his film The Frog Prince and, a while later, her work for the BBC series Celts sowed the seeds of the multi-layered vocal sound which featured so prominently on her hit album "Watermark" in 1988.

That style has become all-important to her, and she sees her voice as merely a part of the music overall - which is why she is so passionate about singing in Gaelic, Latin and English. And why she is so surprised when people comment on how unusual that is.

"My voice is an instrument," she shrugs. "The language of the piano is not in question - why should I restrict my voice to one form?"

Far more intriguing for Enya is the prospect of listening to other people's music - that is something which she has great difficulty in understanding, whatever tongue it's sung in.

"It frightens me. It scares me because I think I'm in the wrong business if that's the type of music the public wants..."

Enya's "Watermark" album produced the most unusual Network Chart Number One of the year – "Orinoco Flow".

CHARLES SPEAKS OUT

"Life begins at 40" said the badge Prince Charles wore for his birthday celebrations on November 14 and, as if to prove the slogan true, he started living it as he means to go on; by speaking his mind.

The future King commenced his 41st year with the controversy surrounding his outspoken views on British architecture still clamouring all around him. Always a fierce defender of traditional structures - and a candid critic of so many new buildings - the Prince had succeeded in attacking the architects once again with a television documentary, A Vision of Britain. In it, his royal highness was seen travelling the length of Britain and ridiculing some of the most famous landmarks in the country.

He considered that the Royal National Theatre situated on the South Bank of the capital's River Thames seemed "like a clever way of building a nuclear power station in the middle of London without anyone objecting." He suggested that "it took 300 years after The Great Fire of London to build the city, and 15 years to destroy it." He spoke of "somewhat godforsaken cities" with "their hearts torn out and thrown away" - and he upset a lot of people.

As with his previous comments about "the rape of Britain" or his famous dismissal of a proposed extension to the National Gallery in Trafalgar Square as a "monstrous carbuncle," the regal campaigner demolished his relationship with many architects. Yet, as surveys have since shown, the public seems to be on his side in the crusade to build a Britain which is pleasing to the eye. A poll conducted after his TV programme showed that 80 per cent of those questioned 'approved strongly' of his views on protecting our environment.

And to those who did not, the Prince had this to say: "This is very much the age of the computer and the word processor - but why on earth do we have to be surrounded by buildings that look like machines...?"

(SYNDICATION INTERNATIONAL)

Prince Charles displays the Royal dental work.

SENNA CLINCHES CHAMPIONSHIP TITLE

Ever since his very first appearance on the track as a Formula One racing car driver, Ayrton Senna has been earmarked as a future world champion.

His debut in the big league came on native soil, at the Brazilian Grand Prix in 1984, and a little over four years later all the predictions - and his life-long dream - had come true. Senna drove to victory so convincingly in 1988 that he had already lifted the World Championship crown before November's Australian Grand Prix, the final race of the season. And the 28-year-old from Sao Paolo also powered to a succession of racing landmarks along the way including a best-ever championship point total of 87, a matchless feat of 13 pole positions in one season - and a record total of eight wins.

The statistics have been the product of Senna's single-minded determination to be the best, a burning ambition which revealed itself to him first when his wealthy businessman father placed him at the wheel of a 12 miles per hour go-kart at the age of four. Since then, Senna has steadily progressed through the gears and racing levels - but his rise to the top has cost him his marriage and a normal existence.

Senna is simply devoted to his sport - "There is no room in my life for anything but cars," he says - and he is not worried that his desire to take the chequered flag first has won him few friends. Indeed, on one particular occasion his arrogant behaviour so upset Nigel Mansell that Britain's number one driver dragged Senna from his car - and the pair almost came to blows.

"When the competition starts, it's every man for himself," Senna says of his approach to racing. "The amount of money behind the Formula One circus is so high that no one could care less about anything else. I'm in Formula One to be a winner!"

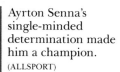

Ayrton Senna's single-minded determination made him a champion.
(ALLSPORT)

TOP 10 MUSIC VIDEOS

1	1	THE LEGEND CONTINUES	Michael Jackson	(Motown/Video Collection)
2	5	THE MAKING OF 'THRILLER'	Michael Jackson	(Vestron)
3	2	SIGN O' THE TIMES	Prince	(Palace)
4	4	LIVE	Belinda Carlisle	(Virgin)
5	8	NOW THAT'S WHAT I CALL MUSIC 12	Various	(PMI/Virgin)
6	7	THE VIDEO SINGLES	Wet Wet Wet	(Channel 5)
7	12	HISTORIA	Def Leppard	(Polygram Music Video)
8	NEW	VOLUME 2	Genesis	(Virgin)
9	6	TANGO IN THE NIGHT	Fleetwood Mac	(WEA)
10	16	UNDER A BLOOD RED SKY	U2	(Virgin)

TOP 20 ALBUMS

1	2	MONEY FOR NOTHING	Dire Straits	(Vertigo)
2	1	RATTLE & HUM	U2	(Island)
3	7	ANY LOVE	Luther Vandross	(Epic)
4	6	KYLIE	Kylie Minogue	(PWL)
5	10	WATERMARK	Enya	(WEA)
6	3	INTROSPECTIVE	Pet Shop Boys	(Parlophone)
7	5	THE BEST OF CHRIS REA - NEW LIGHT THROUGH OLD WINDOWS	Chris Rea	(WEA)
8	NEW	RAGE	T'Pau	(Siren)
9	13	GIVING YOU THE BEST THAT I GOT	Anita Baker	(Elektra)
10	4	THE GREATEST HITS COLLECTION	Bananarama	(London)
11	56	SMASH HITS PARTY '88	Various	(Chrysalis)
12	8	TO WHOM IT MAY CONCERN	Pasadenas	(CBS)
13	12	FLYING COLOURS	Chris De Burgh	(A&M)
14	41	THE GREATEST LOVE	Various	(Telstar)
15	11	REVOLUTIONS	Jean Michel Jarre	(Polydor)
16	30	THE INNOCENTS	Erasure	(Mute)
17	19	FISHERMAN'S BLUES	Waterboys	(Chrysalis)
18	14	CONSCIENCE	Womack & Womack	(4th & Broadway)
19	24	ANCIENT HEART	Tanita Tikaram	(WEA)
20	21	TRACY CHAPMAN	Tracy Chapman	(Elektra)

TOP 10 SINGLES

WEEK 2

1	1	ORINOCO FLOW (SAIL AWAY)	Enya	(WEA)
2	2	JE NE SAIS PAS POURQUOI	Kylie Minogue	(PWL)
3	3	STAND UP FOR YOUR LOVE RIGHTS	Yazz & The Plastic Population	(Big Life)
4	6	GIRL YOU KNOW IT'S TRUE	Milli Vanilli	(Cooltempo)
5	5	KISS	Art Of Noise featuring Tom Jones	(China)
6	19	THE FIRST TIME	Robin Beck	(Mercury)
7	8	SHE MAKES MY DAY	Robert Palmer	(EMI)
8	4	WE CALL IT ACIEED	D. Mob	(London)
9	13	REAL GONE KID	Deacon Blue	(CBS)
10	11	CAN YOU PARTY	Royal House	(Champion)

WEEK 3

1	6	THE FIRST TIME	Robin Beck	(Mercury)
2	1	ORINOCO FLOW (SAIL AWAY)	Enya	(WEA)
3	15	HE AIN'T NO COMPETITION	Brother Beyond	(Parlophone)
4	3	STAND UP FOR YOUR LOVE RIGHTS	Yazz & The Plastic Population	(Big Life)
5	11	1-2-3	Gloria Estefan & The Miami Sound Machine	(Epic)
6	2	JE NE SAIS PAS POURQUOI	Kylie Minogue	(PWL)
7	18	MISSING YOU	Chris De Burgh	(A&M)
8	4	GIRL YOU KNOW IT'S TRUE	Milli Vanilli	(Cooltempo)
9	7	SHE MAKES MY DAY	Robert Palmer	(EMI)
10	17	LET'S STICK TOGETHER	Bryan Ferry	(E.G.)

WEEK 4

1	1	THE FIRST TIME	Robin Beck	(Mercury)
2	11	NEED YOU TONIGHT	INXS	(Mercury)
3	3	HE AIN'T NO COMPETITION	Brother Beyond	(Parlophone)
4	4	STAND UP FOR YOUR LOVE RIGHTS	Yazz & The Plastic Population	(Big Life)
5	7	MISSING YOU	Chris De Burgh	(A&M)
6	14	TWIST AND SHOUT	Salt 'n' Pepa	(London)
7	6	JE NE SAIS PAS POURQUOI	Kylie Minogue	(PWL)
8	2	ORINOCO FLOW (SAIL AWAY)	Enya	(WEA)
9	15	THE CLAIRVOYANT	Iron Maiden	(EMI)
10	17	TIL I LOVED YOU	Barbra Streisand & Don Johnson	(CBS)

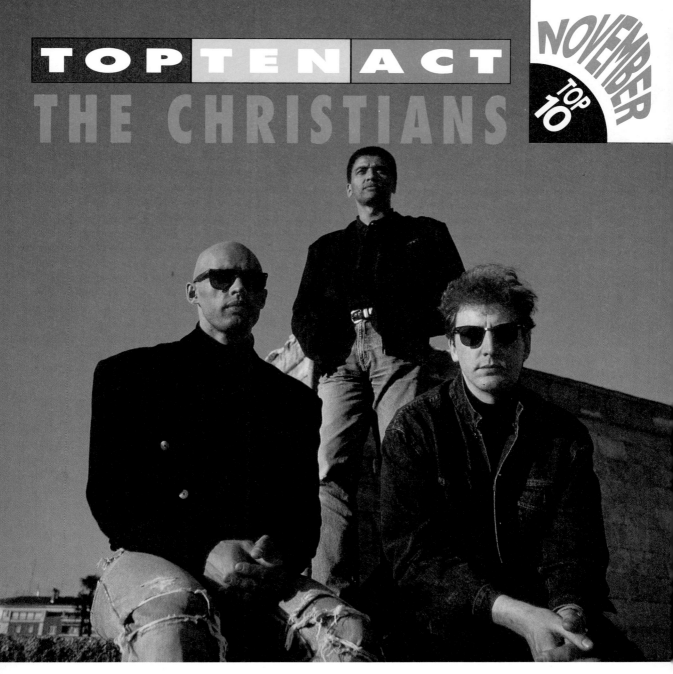

TOP TEN ACT
THE CHRISTIANS

As The Christians' keyboard player, Henry Priestman, pointed out at the time, "Harvest For The World" was a record which people could choose whether or not to buy - but those for whom it was made had no choices left in life.

Proceeds from sales of "Harvest For The World" went to help the millions affected each year by catastrophes around the world. The Disasters Emergency Committee is the organisation providing the aid following the Network Chart Top Ten success of the single.

"Harvest For The World" came about after four animation companies got together to make a video for the song and approached The Christians to record it. The suggestion that the Liverpool group should become involved was one which singer Garry immediately had serious misgivings about.

"I was as chuffed as anything, I mean, I was... humbled to get involved with such a cause," he explains, "but the song is such a great one anyway. I thought 'How can we do this justice? Why don't they release it as it is - the way The Isley Brothers originally did it in 1976?'"

In the event, The Christians actually took the song higher in the charts than it had ever gone before and earned themselves a sixth successive hit - along with some badly needed cash for a worthy cause.

Formed in the early Eighties, The Christians released their self-titled first album in October 1987 - the biggest-selling debut album in the history of Island Records - and a year later it was still on the chart. The band allowed themselves a few celebratory drinks to toast the anniversary, but fame and acclaim is not something with which they would normally bother themselves. Their no-nonsense Liverpool attitude would never allow it, says Garry.

"I think that's what it is. I mean, all Liverpudlians are the same, basically - they'll have a laugh, but they don't like getting messed about. They don't like getting trod on or walked over in any way."

DECEMBER

NESCAFÉ **THE NETWORK CHART SHOW**

▶ NETWORK CHART TOP 40 ◀

1	25	MISTLETOE AND WINE............**Cliff Richard** ....(EMI)
2	14	CAT AMONG THE PIGEONS/SILENT NIGHT.......**Bros**................................(CBS)
3	21	SUDDENLY............................**Angry Anderson** ....(Food For Thought)
4	1	FIRST TIME.......................**Robin Beck** ....(Mercury)
5	3	LEFT TO MY OWN DEVICES....**Pet Shop Boys** ....(Parlophone)
6	NEW	ESPECIALLY FOR YOU.............**Kylie Minogue & Jason Donovan** ....(PWL)
7	5	TWO HEARTS.........................**Phil Collins** ....(Virgin)
8	9	SAY A LITTLE PRAYER...**Bomb The Bass featuring Maureen** ......(Rhythm King)
9	7	SMOOTH CRIMINAL................**Michael Jackson** ....(Epic)
10	8	TAKE ME TO YOUR HEART .....**Rick Astley**..(RCA)
11	4	MISSING YOU........................**Chris De Burgh** ....(A&M)
12	18	STAKKER HUMANOID..............**Humanoid** ....(Westside)
13	2	NEED YOU TONIGHT ....**INXS** ....(Mercury)
14	19	JACK TO THE SOUND OF THE UNDERGROUND.....**Hithouse** ....(Supreme)
15	16	RADIO ROMANCE...................**Tiffany** ....(MCA)
16	NEW	CRACKERS INTERNATIONAL EP.............**Erasure** ....(Mute)
17	29	KISSING A FOOL.....................**George Michael** ....(Epic)
18	6	TWIST AND SHOUT ....**Salt 'n' Pepa** ....(London)
19	13	NATHAN JONES...................**Bananarama** ....(London)
20	26	KOKOMO ....**Beach Boys** ....(Elektra)
21	48	BURNING BRIDGES (ON AND OFF AND ON AGAIN)...........**Status Quo** ....(Vertigo)
22	NEW	FINE TIME ....**New Order** ....(Factory)
23	15	REAL GONE KID....................**Deacon Blue** ....(CBS)
24	32	DOWNTOWN '88....................**Petula Clark** ....(PRT)
25	12	HE AIN'T NO COMPETITION....**Brother Beyond** ....(Parlophone)
26	35	ENCHANTED LADY.................**Pasadenas** ....(CBS)
27	10	STAND UP FOR YOUR LOVE RIGHTS...**Yazz & The Plastic Population** (Big Life)
28	17	JE NE SAIS PAS POURQUOI....**Kylie Minogue** ....(PWL)
29	41	YOU ARE THE ONE ....**A-ha** ....(Warner Brothers)
30	24	GIRL YOU KNOW IT'S TRUE...**Milli Vanilli** ....(Cooltempo)
31	37	LOVE HOUSE.........................**Samantha Fox** ....(Jive)
32	11	THE CLAIRVOYANT.................**Iron Maiden** ....(EMI)
33	45	9 A.M. ....**London Beat** ....(Anxious)
34	NEW	BORN TO BE MY BABY...........**Bon Jovi** ....(Vertigo)
35	61	LOCO IN ACAPULCO..............**Four Tops** ....(Arista)
36	59	FOUR LETTER WORD.............**Kim Wilde** ....(MCA)
37	20	ORINOCO FLOW (SAIL AWAY)......**Enya** ....(WEA)
38	31	1-2-3.................**Gloria Estefan & The Miami Sound Machine** ....(Epic)
39	46	ROAD TO OUR DREAM...........**T'Pau** ....(Siren)
40	NEW	GOOD LIFE................................**Inner City** ....(10)

Phil Collins

(RETNA)

Beach Boys

(RETNA)

CLIFF RICHARD

Harry Rodger Webb was 15 years old when he realised for the first time that he wanted to be someone else - Elvis Presley.

The discovery came suddenly and without warning one day as he walked through the streets of Waltham Cross and happened to hear a blast of Presley singing "Heartbreak Hotel" on the radio of a passing car - and just four years later the Indian-born boy began the most remarkable chart run in the history of British pop music. By then, of course, he had become another person!

Though the press were happy to seize the obvious opportunity of dubbing him 'Britain's answer to Elvis', Harry had reinvented himself by another title. He called himself Cliff Richard. Cliff has continued to have hits ever since his very first smash, "Move It", reached number two back in 1958.

In December, 1988, his 99th release became his 11th solo number one, "Mistletoe and Wine" - an appropriate success in the year of his 30th anniversary as a major star. During that time, 48-year-old Cliff has amassed a matchless procession of statistical landmarks. He has spent more weeks in the Top 30 - 1009 at the time of his Christmas chart-topper - than the Beatles, Abba, Madonna and Whitney Houston have managed between them. He is the only artist to have scored hit singles with new material in both the UK and US during the Fifties, Sixties, Seventies and Eighties. He has recorded 43 hit albums, of which 27 made the Top Ten. He was one of the earliest British artists to debut at number one, doing so in 1962 with the "The Young Ones". And he is still not satisfied.

"I am surprised I've lasted so long, because anything over five years is a bonus in this industry," he admits, "and no one else has drummed up three hit singles every year for 30 years. But there are plenty of challenges still left."

Such as? "Everything again, really - and better. I mean, you can never, having made one record, really say that it's sufficient. You want to make a second one. If you get a gold disc, you want two gold discs. For me, though, the real pleasure of my career has been that I've left everybody with question marks over their heads all the time - because no one can say that I only record one type of song."

Indeed, aside from the varied nature of many of his solo singles, Cliff has also recorded diverse hits with people including Elton John, Phil Everly, Sarah Brightman and The Young Ones - whose success with a madcap version of "Living Doll" in 1986 was another number one for Cliff - his 12th overall. And his 100th hit came this year (1989) with a further partnership with Aswad.

"One of my pet hates is that people will write me off as being bland and predictable," he shrugs, "and I'm not in the least predictable. I couldn't be less so, I'd have thought. So this career is all fun for me because I know that a lot of people have their own idea of what rock 'n' roll is - and I fly in the face of all that and say 'You're wrong. You don't have to be like that.' Rock 'n' roll can't be tied down to a particular type."

With his clean-living, eternally youthful image, Cliff does indeed appear poles apart from Anthrax, or even Tom Jones, but he has never let that hold him back. "I'm flattered when people say 'Don't you think you're too good to be true?' But it worries me that it's meant as a criticism," says Cliff, a practising Christian.

"And, of course, I've been mocked and sniggered at sometimes because of my religious beliefs. So, OK, not eveyone likes me - but I must have something..."

After 30 years in showbiz Cliff won a "Brit" award for a lifetime's dedication to the industry and now he wants to do it all again.

(RETNA)

(ASSOCIATED PRESS)

The crater gouged out of the earth in Lockerbie by the stricken 747.

DOOMED JET DEVASTATES LOCKERBIE

As it flew towards the Atlantic at 7.19 pm, 31,000 ft up and cruising at a speed of 550 mph, Flight PA 103 suddenly vanished from the radar screens of the Scottish Air Traffic Control in Prestwick.

There had been no Mayday or distress call from the pilot, whose last radio message had come just four minutes earlier, but when the plane appeared again on that tragic evening of 21 December, Britain's worst ever air disaster had devastated the quiet town of Lockerbie in Scotland. En route from London to New York, the Pan Am Boeing 747 jumbo jet plummetted from the skies at the rate of 4,000 ft per minute killing all 258 people on board - 243 passengers and 15 crew.

Their bodies rained down with the wreckage of the aircraft, parts of which were found as far as 50 miles from Lockerbie. A

further 17 lives were claimed on the ground where the debris came to rest. Houses were flattened, cars gutted, buildings blitzed and a 30 ft deep burning crater was scooped from the earth by the fallen wreck.

In the aftermath of the mysterious incident, two theories immediately presented themselves; either the plane had crashed because of a fault, or it had been destroyed by design. Exactly a week later, following many hours of brilliant detective work by Ministry of Defence scientists, the latter was confirmed. An explosive device had been carefully and clinically smuggled into the luggage hold of the doomed jet.

As soon as the news broke, several terrorist organisations quickly claimed responsibility for the act of planting the powerful bomb, but for the dead and the bereaved they left behind, the question was not who did it - but why?

On both sides of the Atlantic, Christmas 1988 was to be a very bleak time indeed for the friends and relatives of the Pan Am passengers and the little town of Lockerbie.

(ALLSPORT)

BRUNO V TYSON?

British boxing fans saw it as the fight of the century, Frank Bruno saw it as the chance of a lifetime, but undisputed World Heavyweight Boxing Champion Mike Tyson saw it all as a bit of an inconvenience.

The Bruno/Tyson clash had originally been planned for September 3 and Bruno had worked hard for this, his second crack at the world title. In December he seemed set to seize his chance - if only Tyson would let him.

The fight had been cancelled, rescheduled, postponed and reorganised amid a barrage of arguments over money, dates and venues, but the biggest stumbling block of all for the fight organisers was Mike Tyson's rather public private life. Tyson's personal problems were leaving Bruno tangled in the ropes - it seemed like the two boxers would never step into the ring together!

Breaking his hand in a 4 a.m Harlem street brawl would have been a major embarassment to any other World Champion due to defend his title but for Tyson it was just another minor headache to add to his growing catalogue of catastrophes.

He was embroiled in a bitter dispute with the men who had

been managing his fight career and his financial affairs.

His wife of just a few months, television actress Robin Givens, had told millions of TV viewers that life with Tyson was unbearable and that he was bad tempered and violent - a brave thing to say when her bad tempered, violent husband was sitting right next to her at the time!

Driving alone on a mountain road, Tyson managed to achieve what no other boxer in the world had done - he knocked out Mike Tyson. True, even he needed a BMW and a large tree to do it, but after the crash he was out cold for twenty minutes and admitted to hospital.

Tyson's wife, who claimed to have had a miscarriage, started divorce proceedings, suing for over £25 million. Tyson fought back with a claim that Robin had tricked him into marrying her. She finally dropped her action after readers of popular newspapers voted her the most hated woman in America - not the most desirable qualification for a TV actress.

Meanwhile Frank Bruno worked steadfastly on his training programme, suffering each new delay with good humour. By now, he was talking about crossing the Atlantic to fight Tyson like most people would talk about crossing the road to the chip shop. He'd had his own problems, however. On holiday in Jamaica with his family he'd been hit by a hurricane - probably the best training he could get for dealing with Tyson!

Tyson still didn't seem too concerned by Bruno's burning desire to knock his block off and turned his attention to religion instead. He was baptised in Cleveland by Jesse Jackson.

December's news that the fight would definitely go ahead in early '89 saw Bruno jetting off to the States once more and despite Tyson's new-found piety and Bruno's own religious beliefs, one thing was certain - neither would be showing much Christian charity when the bell finally went for the start of round one!

ABOVE: Frank Bruno
RIGHT: Mike Tyson

(ALLSPORT)

TOP TEN BEST SELLING SINGLES OF 1988

1	THE ONLY WAY IS UP	Yazz & The Plastic Population	(Big Life)
2	I SHOULD BE SO LUCKY	Kylie Minogue	(PWL)
3	MISTLETOE AND WINE	Cliff Richard	(EMI)
4	I THINK WE'RE ALONE NOW	Tiffany	(MCA)
5	NOTHING'S GONNA CHANGE MY LOVE FOR YOU	Glenn Medeiros	(London)
6	ESPECIALLY FOR YOU	Kylie Minogue & Jason Donovan	(PWL)
7	WITH A LITTLE HELP FROM MY FRIENDS	Wet Wet Wet/	
	SHE'S LEAVING HOME	Billy Bragg	(Childline)
8	LOCOMOTION	Kylie Minogue	(PWL)
9	HE AIN'T HEAVY HE'S MY BROTHER	The Hollies	(EMI)
10	TEARDROPS	Womack & Womack	(4th & Broadway)

TOP TEN BEST SELLING ALBUMS OF 1988

1	KYLIE	Kylie Minogue	(PWL)
2	NOW THAT'S WHAT I CALL MUSIC XIII	Various	(EMI/Virgin/Polygram)
3	POPPED IN SOULED OUT	Wet Wet Wet	(Precious Organisation)
4	MONEY FOR NOTHING	Dire Straits	(Vertigo)
5	THE HARDLINE ACCORDING TO	Terence Trent D'Arby	(CBS)
6	TRACY CHAPMAN	Tracy Chapman	(Elektra)
7	BAD	Michael Jackson	(Epic)
8	TANGO IN THE NIGHT	Fleetwood Mac	(Warner Brothers)
9	RATTLE AND HUM	U2	(Island)
10	NOW THAT'S WHAT I CALL MUSIC 12	Various	(EMI/Virgin/Polygram)

Never mind the telly, or the papers, RADIO is the music medium. Radio is the fun medium and you can take it with you wherever you go, whatever you are doing.

Independent Radio has more music and more fun than any other radio. That's why it's the radio for young listeners EVERYWHERE.

There are Independent Radio stations all over the British Isles. They're part of the same system, but every one has its own personality, its own style, its own music choice.

That style and choice is right for YOU, wherever you are, because Independent Radio stations know music and know what young people want to hear. They're also in tune with the areas they serve, so when you tune in to your local Independent Radio station you won't hear a D.J. who has never set foot in one of your local clubs droning on about people and places you've never seen. He'll be talking about what's new and news in YOUR area.

Independent Radio is itself young – just 15 years old. It began with just one or two stations – Capital in London, Clyde in Glasgow, Piccadilly in Manchester, Metro in Newcastle, and so on. But we have gone on adding new stations, new sounds, new voices and personalities and LOTS MORE MUSIC every year.

Now there are 49 Independent Radio stations in England, Scotland, Wales and Northern Ireland and there are loads more on the way! Independent Radio has been told by the Government that from 1990 onwards there will be many more spots on the dial for Independent Radio stations. So lots of groups are lining up to run these stations and there will be many exciting opportunities for young people to broadcast on as well as listen to INDEPENDENT RADIO.